The Rise of Tourism on
MARTHA'S VINEYARD

D1287469

THE RISE OF TOURISM ON
MARTHA'S VINEYARD

THOMAS DRESSER

FOREWORD BY NANCY GARDELLA
DIRECTOR OF THE MARTHA'S VINEYARD CHAMBER OF COMMERCE

THE
History
PRESS

Published by The History Press
Charleston, SC
www.historypress.com

Copyright © 2020 by Thomas Dresser
All rights reserved

First published 2020

Manufactured in the United States

ISBN 9781467143370

Library of Congress Control Number: 2020931993

Notice: The information in this book is true and complete to the best of our knowledge. It is offered without guarantee on the part of the author or The History Press. The author and The History Press disclaim all liability in connection with the use of this book.

All rights reserved. No part of this book may be reproduced or transmitted in any form whatsoever without prior written permission from the publisher except in the case of brief quotations embodied in critical articles and reviews.

The Rise of Tourism on Martha's Vineyard is dedicated to Leslie Malcouronne Bunker (1947–2016). For many years Leslie was a spirited bus driver for tourists and school children, always sharing stories, jokes and memories of Vineyard life. Her passing left a huge gap in the tourist industry and the route of the school bus.

CONTENTS

FOREWORD

M y product is Martha's Vineyard," says Nancy Gardella, director of the Martha's Vineyard Chamber of Commerce since 2006. "People dream about coming to the Vineyard." Ms. Gardella relishes her role as chamber director. She is energetic, enthusiastic and excited about the opportunity to promote tourism on Martha's Vineyard. Tourism means jobs.

In 2006, Jon Nelson of Bunch of Grapes said he'd like to know by Labor Day whether he could employ people through Christmas—or even year-round. As Nancy Gardella began her role as director, Mr. Nelson bluntly told her, "Your job is to bring me business outside of July and August. Extend the season."

"Early on, in meeting with businesspeople, we explored the need to extend the season after Labor Day and begin it well before the Fourth of July." She says it's hard to convince people to come to the Vineyard in the winter. And spring often depends on the weather. "The potential for international travelers from Canada, the United Kingdom, western Europe and the Nordic countries to help extend the season is tremendous. They're not dependent on weather, they stay longer and spend more than domestic visitors. And they're willing to visit in spring and fall."

She goes on, "In 2006, town pride and loyalty predominated; the chamber struggled to unite towns under one Martha's Vineyard banner."

Martha's Vineyard has been designated by the state as a regional tourism council, which means it is responsible for destination marketing for the island. The State of Massachusetts invests in tourism marketing, but the amount varies year to year. And tourism is definitely a cash cow. "Our job is to promote Martha's Vineyard," she says, raving about the recent successful summer season. "We had 96 percent occupancy last summer—huge house rental market. I believe anyone with a job on Martha's Vineyard is at most separated by two degrees from the tourism industry."

She succinctly promotes the importance of visitor spending during the summer: "Forty-five days. That's all summer is, just forty-five days from July 4 to mid-August. Most businesses know that this is a critical time for visitor spending, and despite the strain on their resources, it's critically important to leave a great impression with visitors. Basically, that means be polite and smile." And it works. Customers and tourists who visit Vineyard shops and restaurants are impressed by the courtesy and competence of employees. It's a win-win situation.

"As long as we continue to attract visitors, and they continue to put their heads in our beds and spend their money, then Islanders have jobs and local option tax revenue from room occupancy and meals rolls into our municipalities coffers."

Restaurants like to stay open through December, as do hotels and retailers. Collectively, the fall has been built up. "Our best-kept secret is the success of September through November." She pauses and smiles, "Not so much a secret anymore!" Many locals feel the shoulder season is the best time of year on the Vineyard because of fewer crowds and a calmer atmosphere.

Besides expanding the shoulder season, Nancy Gardella applauds seasonal homeowners, calling them angels. "They are passionately supportive of Martha's Vineyard. They keep our taxes lower. They return to shop. They bring their friends and family to share the Island. They help pay for the police, fire, schools but don't use the services." With their support, they add a great deal to the allure of Martha's Vineyard.

Another benefit to the Island economy and many chamber businesses is weddings. Wedding planning is big business on the Vineyard, as noted by planner Kim Scott: "The variety and number of businesses is extensive, ranging from caterers, tent and rental companies, venues, florists, photographers, videographers, restaurants, bands/DJs/entertainers, bakers, maintenance workers, calligraphers, hair and makeup artists, transportation companies, accommodations and so much more."

Another aspect of tourism is that those people who visit the Vineyard year after year often opt to retire on the Vineyard. Nancy praises Vineyarders who assist homeowners to age in place. The option to remain at home as long as possible is a realistic goal on Martha's Vineyard. The Healthy Aging Task Force offers outreach for people to stay in their homes as long as possible and find architects and contractors to design and build appropriate modifications, such as weather-protected entryways, wheelchair ramps and turning space and adapted furnishings, such as first-floor bedrooms and wider doorways.

The chamber has no need to spend money to promote the Vineyard in the summer—the island sells itself. Ms. Gardella adds, "People have fallen in love with the Vineyard. They contribute to preserve the environment, donate to non-profit organizations, and savor their retirement." Her next goal is to urge Vineyard businesses to start the season earlier. "Tourism equals jobs. We are the economic development corporation."

—Nancy Gardella
Director of the Martha's Vineyard Chamber of Commerce

PREFACE

Native Americans have lived on the Vineyard since before it became an island—when the oceans rose in approximately 3000 BC. Indeed, Indian artifacts date back some ten thousand years, which is corroborated by carbon dating, bone shards and rock fragments.

Through the centuries, the Vineyard has proved to be a site of adventure, excitement and intrigue. That magic contributes to the role of the tourist community today.

We have seen Martha's Vineyard rise in popularity in the last half century, but what led to that? The history of tourism on the Vineyard can be traced through several disparate intervals over the last century and a half—each contributing to the current status, and each individually an influence or cause unto itself.

The first significant group of tourists to venture across the waters to Martha's Vineyard to appreciate the experience were followers of the Methodist Campground community, a religious retreat conducted annually in Oak Bluffs, beginning in 1835. The rapid expansion of this influx of short-term tourists, or revivalists, brought a newfound prominence to the Vineyard, which had been considered a remote outpost without redeeming qualities to entice visitors.

Wesleyan Grove Camp Meeting Association sprang up in the antebellum era and blossomed after the Civil War. Tent-toting Methodists evolved into cottage owners. Tourists and curiosity seekers followed in droves. In the latter half of the nineteenth century, thousands of Methodist advocates joined the ranks for the weeklong summer revival meetings, foregoing the bathing beaches and bars of Oak Bluffs for the soaring oratory of their preachers in the confines of their tabernacle.

A second impact on tourism was the prominent growth of the adjacent Cottage City community. Sparked by the success of the Camp Meeting Association, founders of the Oak Bluffs Land & Wharf Company purchased property adjacent to the campground and proceeded to develop the land into a planned residential community. The goal was to create a town that enticed tourists to the seashore, the adventures of tourism and the attractions of an amusement park atmosphere. And the group was quite successful in its venture. Thus the cottage industry of tourism in Cottage City was born.

Another factor in the rise of tourism on the Vineyard was the decline of the whaling industry. For more than a century, whaling had served as the economic engine of Edgartown and much of the island with its associated jobs. As whaling declined, Edgartown powerbrokers sought a financial replacement. The preponderance of Cottage City tourists led to the construction of the Martha's Vineyard Railroad, designed to encourage tourist traffic to Edgartown. This led to the development of hotels, restaurants and shops—all catering to the tourist trade.

While tourism continued in varying degrees in the first quarter of the twentieth century, the impact of World War II proved an impetus for more Vineyard visitors. The influx of a middle-class African American population was significant following the war. And many military servicemen, stationed on the island during the war, opted to marry local women and settle on Vineyard. All this added to the population. The sense that Martha's Vineyard was no longer an isolated enclave but instead an accessible serene seashore community became popular in the late 1940s. The Vineyard enjoyed a spike in tourists in the postwar era.

More recent influential aspects on tourism involve two bridges and two presidents. It may be specious to lump these four events together, but the impacts are obvious. The incident on the Dike Bridge at Chappaquiddick in 1969 and the Jaws movie by the bridge in 1975 enticed the curious to the Vineyard. That Presidents Clinton and Obama chose to spend their private vacation time on the golf courses and in the restaurants of Martha's Vineyard was definitive proof that the island was a place of prominence, politics and publicity.

Tourists first sought the Vineyard for its isolated beauty and religious respite. Today, tourists visit to see and be seen—to partake in the beauty of the island and revel in the popularity and prominence of this piece of paradise. Time has a way of bringing the Vineyard into the eye of the public and to be desired and devoured, savored and shared, preserved and protected—all at the same time.

ACKNOWLEDGEMENTS

They say it's the journey that makes the trip worthwhile—not solely the destination.

While preparing to write a book, a good deal of planning goes into the preliminary aspects of putting it together—like reviewing the roadmap before a trip. We pack our belongings just as we assemble the research materials, interviews and website links needed to write the book. We set out, full of anticipation, challenged by our daunting task. And once we are on the road, we work diligently to reach our goal, whether it's a warm site in the South or a manuscript ready for publication.

In both cases, the challenge and the pleasure are derived from the experience itself. When the destination has been reached, the book published, it's time to relax and relish the rewards of the adventure. However, the real endeavor, the pleasure-generating but often excruciating experience, is what makes the trip, the book, memorable in the long run.

This is my twelfth book with The History Press—all focused on various historical aspects of Martha's Vineyard. It has taken a dozen years to reach this goal, and along the way, it has been a challenging and gratifying experience. The joy of researching and writing has made this trip so worthwhile.

That said, I want to acknowledge those people who offered direction, advice and suggestions to make this book a reality.

Without my wife, Joyce, photographer, editor, advisor, confidante and suggester-in-chief, I would not have embarked on this adventure. Once again, thanks, Joyce.

Acknowledgements

Hilary Wallcox got me off on the "write" track by suggesting Vineyard Gazette articles on tourism through the years. Thanks, Hilary.

Bow Van Riper at the Martha's Vineyard Museum was a great source of images and encouragement, even as he participated in a major relocation as the museum moved from Edgartown to Vineyard Haven. Thanks, Bow.

Nancy Gardella, director of the Martha's Vineyard Chamber of Commerce, was a great asset as she described the boundaries of tourism on the Vineyard from a business perspective.

Chris Baer offered images that bring the story alive.

Ned Sternick shared information on Daniel Webster's Vineyard visit.

The librarians in Oak Bluffs were of great assistance in researching this topic.

Joan Boykin and Will Jones, childhood summer friends in the Oak Bluffs of years ago, shared their memories.

Kimberly Scott of KG Events added her perspective on Vineyard weddings.

Mike Kinsella at The History Press gave the green light on this venture and was there with the stoplight at the end. Hayley Behal put the finishing touches on the manuscript in preparation for publication.

It is a broad swath of people and places that make the trip a success. Historical researching and writing are not dependent on a single event but a combination of books and articles, suggestions and directions, advice and consent—all of which lend a focus and angle to make a book take shape.

I thank everyone involved for the company they offered on this ride.

—Thomas Dresser
March 11, 2019

FIRST TOURISTS (1640–1835)

The name always attracts attention, and the island is worthy of its name.[1]
—Pocket Directory Guide

The Wampanoag, known as people of the first light, were the first to venture to Martha's Vineyard. Curious, adventuresome and appreciative of the area, this Native American band settled on the land thousands of years ago.

The Wampanoag people consider the Vineyard their home as they have for thousands of years, well before the white man first visited. The Wampanoag have lived on this land for ten thousand years, based on archaeological artifacts such as carbon-dated settlements, bones, stone tools and trade artifacts.

Geologically, a pair of glacial lobes descended from the north on either side of the Vineyard triangle. The Buzzards Bay glacier created the western terminal moraine with rich soil, kettle ponds, lots of rocks and glacial erratics. The Cape Cod glacier formed the eastern Great Plains, depositing quantities of sand and gravel, which constitute the bulk of the central Vineyard landmass. Sea levels dropped as the glaciers settled over the land.

Eons later, as the glaciers melted, the ocean waters rose. Five thousand years ago, the glaciers receded and melted. Ocean waters flooded the land around the Vineyard, cutting it off from the mainland. That created the island of Martha's Vineyard.

Thus was born what the Wampanoag called Noepe, or "land amid the waters," a perfect description of an island. Even the first occupants, the Wampanoag, were on island before it became an island. Everyone who followed could be labeled a tourist, visitor, washashore or off-islander. The only natives are the Native Americans.

The Wampanoag settled near freshwater sources in various sites around the Vineyard—closer to the ocean in the summer and withdrawing inland in the cooler months. Three distinct settlements have been uncovered that were in constant use nearly eight thousand years. One site is near Squibnocket, once open to the ocean as determined by middens or piles of seashells. That settlement included the area from Mill Brook to Stonewall Pond and Menemsha. Another area ranged from Edgartown Great Pond and Katama out to Cape Poge and Sengekontacket. A third Native American settlement spread west from the Lagoon to Lake Tashmoo.

Archaeological research determined that natives lived in "family groups that were highly mobile and organized around natural resources that varied in availability and location throughout the year." As the earliest tourists, natives explored their surroundings, venturing to nearby islands and across to the mainland, yet lived year-round in the area. Seasonal changes in their food supply caused them to move away from the shore in cooler weather and then return to live by the ocean in the warmer months.[2]

The first white man to visit the Vineyard documented his travels. Bartholomew Gosnold sailed from Falmouth, England, in 1602 with two goals: develop a colony in the New World and harvest enough sassafras to make his venture worthwhile. He failed at the former and succeeded at the latter. (Additionally, he sought gold and searched for the lost colony of Roanoke, neither successfully.) Bartholomew Gosnold never set foot on Martha's Vineyard, although he is credited with naming the island, ostensibly for his mother-in-law, Martha Golden, who financed his expedition.

The journals of John Brererton and Gabriel Archer, two diarists aboard Gosnold's ship, were published on the return of the Concord in 1602 and were most likely read by William Shakespeare, who penned The Tempest in 1610. Whether or not The Tempest is based on Gosnold's exploits on Martha's Vineyard is immaterial to a great legend. The first Vineyard tourists were Captain Bartholomew Gosnold and his crew.

In 1642, the first village was settled on Martha's Vineyard by Thomas Mayhew Jr., his father and their followers.[3] It was initially known as Great Harbour. The early economy was based on farming and fishing. The village was later named Edgartown in honor of the son of James, the Duke of

York. Young Edgar died at four years old in 1666. The Duke of York went on to become King James II. "Over the course of the late 19th and early 20th centuries, Edgartown reinvented itself as a summer-centered community of resort hotels, bathing beaches, and genteel vacation homes." It became the county seat of Dukes County, which referenced the Duke of York. Furthermore, "Edgartown as summer vacation spot, welcomed the world to its shores." One could consider Edgartown the prim and proper host of the burgeoning resort community.[4]

Two other Vineyard settlements were settled by white men in the mid-seventeenth century: Chilmark and Tisbury. The rich soil proved good for farming along the terminal moraine up-island; the vast acreage was available for raising sheep, which produced both wool and lamb for Chilmark farmers. The down-island settlement of Holmes Hole (later Vineyard Haven in Tisbury) offered a sheltered harbor for ships passing through Vineyard Sound—a haven for fishing and merchant vessels in storms. These three settlements were linked by rustic roadways, but, as David Foster points out, "Travel from one to another meant crossing somewhat desolate stretches of scrub and woods on frequently miserable roadways that were regularly disparaged in contemporary accounts."[5]

Although the island was isolated, people from the mainland still visited the Vineyard on occasion. John Adams is said to have traveled to Chilmark in 1760 to visit college classmate Jonathan Allen. Horse-drawn carriages faced challenges on the rustic roadways. In 1838, it was reported that one traveler journeyed from West Tisbury out to Gay Head and faced opening and closing thirty fence gates along the way. The fenced-in landscape kept sheep in pastureland but slowed travel. The first tourists faced myriad hurdles in getting around.

Early on, the Vineyard earned a reputation as a welcoming place to outsiders. Intrepid travelers appreciated the friendly nature and hospitality of the local populace. Vineyarders did not assume airs; they showed visitors where to go and what to see in a friendly manner while they went about their daily tasks of fishing and farming. That acceptance of tourists has been a hallmark of Vineyarders through the years, with only minimal exceptions.

The Vineyard Gazette began operations in 1846 and soon investigated the opportunities afforded tourists who wanted to sample life on Martha's Vineyard. A vacation destination was termed a watering place and such sites included Saratoga Springs, New York, and Newport, Rhode Island. The Vineyard offered a unique setting, something different—an island locality.

An early Gazette article sought to promote the Vineyard to allow "the gentleman of leisure to enjoy himself here, on good old Martha's Vineyard." In comparing the Vineyard to Newport, the Gazette considered the beaches to be far superior on island. And the magnificent view of Vineyard Sound should not be missed. Scan out onto the Atlantic to watch the New York to Liverpool mailboats steam by. "A more beautiful sight is seldom seen than a fleet of one or two hundred sail of vessels under weigh at the same time, by moonlight."[6]

And the fishing! Oh, my. "From the blue-fish, perch and striped bass, to the boneto [sic] and swordfish," the article boasted, "there are no places in New England, that will compare with us for a moment, in the pursuit and taking of fish." It was noted that "better oysters cannot be found" than in Vineyard oyster beds. Additionally, "our beautiful creek, named in honor of the Matakesett tribe of Indians, with its sparkling waters," offers an abundance of plentiful alewife.

Casual horseback riding through quaint villages, past great stands of trees with appealing vistas, was promoted as a delightful way to enjoy the environment. It was recommended that the prospective visitor journey out to Gay Head, where the cliffs are majestic, and seashells, shark teeth and fossils may be uncovered in the clay cliffs. And don't miss the surf at South Beach, especially after a storm has blasted across the land.

"Nature has done everything for us that we would require,—has showered her blessings around us in the richest profusion," the Gazette writer boasted. Even access to the Vineyard was delightful. The captain who operated steamship service from New Bedford was endowed with "no blustering and self-conceited airs, everything is pleasant and generous to a fault with him."

The final caveat clinched the argument that the Vineyard was the place to visit: "We must know the Vineyard possesses advantages equal, if not superior, to any watering place in New England; this is no idle remark."

Yet the author acknowledged a need to be amended: "I am well convinced that, nothing more is required to make our island a resort for the savant, the gentleman of pleasure, as well the invalid, but a first class, well conducted hotel." While the Vineyard was viewed by that author as a superior watering place, it would benefit from a commodious hotel, "a plain, substantial edifice, suitable to accommodate one hundred persons." The article made a strong argument for visitors to vacation and tour the Vineyard.

One erstwhile politician who was known across the country made a pilgrimage to the Vineyard in the summer of 1849. Massachusetts senator Daniel Webster arrived unannounced and made an impact.

The Vineyard Gazette did announce Daniel Webster's visit on August 9, 1849. Titled Distinguished Guests, the article noted Senator Daniel Webster "went blue-fishing on Tuesday, and caught two-thirds of the fish taken, notwithstanding he was accompanied by extra fishermen. Mr. Webster, we learn, will remain here till Saturday, previous to which time it is his intention to visit the far-famed promontory of Gay Head." The senator did ride out to Gay Head in a carriage with the most prominent Vineyarder of the day, whale oil magnate Dr. Daniel Fisher. The two men enjoyed the "opportunity for plover shooting, as well as snipe and grouse."

Ecologist David Foster assessed Webster's visit, observing, "Most notably, the future of the island as a great leisure destination began to glimmer with the arrival of such national figures as Daniel Webster (1849) and Nathaniel Hawthorne (1850) both of whom included plover hunting with leading businessman Dr. Daniel Fisher on their itinerary."[7]

With their Vineyard visits, Webster and Hawthorne recognized Martha's Vineyard as a potential tourist destination, just as the Wampanoag had appreciated it thousands of years earlier. And the Gazette was justifiably proud of Webster's visit, concluding its piece by noting, "Of course, quite a number of pleasure-seekers will follow in the wake of these distinguished statesmen."

The tourist bonanza was underway.

WESLEYAN GROVE (1835–65)

Theunprecedentedpopularityof theMartha'sVineyardCampMeetingprovedto
themindsof somepublicspiritedgentlementheeasewithwhichthispartof the
islandmightbemadethemostpopularsummerresortinallNewEngland.[8]
—Guide of Cottage City

W hen Jeremiah Pease founded the camp meeting association, he recognized the potential of the Vineyard as a place of peaceful tranquility removed from the hustle of humanity.

Reverend Pease selected a remote grove of oak trees on the shores of Squash Meadow Pond in Oak Bluffs as a meeting place for a Methodist revival community. The year was 1835. The site was removed from the mainland and more than a mile from the tiny settlement of Eastville, on Vineyard Haven harbor. It was inaccessible by boat. Reaching Wesleyan Grove required riding along a rustic road of six to eight miles from either Edgartown or Vineyard Haven. Nevertheless, the first preacher at Wesleyan Grove opened the first Methodist service on August 24, 1835, with nine families tenting beneath the protective canopy of an oak grove. The tiny settlement became an outpost of the Methodist revival movement.

JOHN WESLEY FOUNDED METHODISM in England in the mid-1700s. The focus of Methodism was a deep and specific concern with the inequities of society.

Wesley rode a circuit across England, preaching to the impoverished that they could be saved. He spoke to his congregants with hope, offering an option to the conventional Congregationalist theology of original sin and eternal damnation. With the establishment of the United States in the late eighteenth century, "implicitly democratic, Methodism was the right thing at the right time for the new American nation."[9]

John Saunders, an escaped slave, first introduced the new religion to the Vineyard in 1787. Later, one of Wesley's ministers, Reverend Jesse Lee, visited the Vineyard.

The Camp Meeting movement began nationally in 1799 in Kentucky. While various denominations advocated revivalism through the camp meeting, it was the Methodists who promoted the retreat most ardently. Three common tenets of the Methodist theology prevailed during this early era of growth: abolition of slavery, support for women and temperance. In many ways, the nineteenth-century Methodist movement was ahead of its time.

Methodist revivalism swept the northeast United States in the nineteenth century with tent cities popping up in virtually every state. A partial list of Camp Meeting communities includes Plainville Campgrounds in Connecticut; Empire Grove in Poland, Maine; Asbury Grove in Hamilton, Massachusetts; Advent Christian Campground in Alton Bay, New Hampshire; Portsmouth Camp Meeting in New Hampshire; Ocean Grove, New Jersey; Rehoboth Beach, Delaware; Round Lake, New York; Mount Gretna, Pennsylvania; and East Barnard, Vermont.

As Methodists emigrated from England to America, itinerant ministers rode the circuit in a regular route along the eastern part of land, stopping at each village and preaching to the poor. John Wesley and his disciples sought to convert the invalid, the pauper and the impoverished to the rebirth of religion through the Methodist Church.

Methodism spread across the Vineyard. Leaders of other denominations welcomed the new faith. The Vineyard's Jonathan Mayhew led his Congregational followers to the cusp of Unitarianism, which extolled the virtues of the intellect and preached that salvation depended on individual character. Mayhew recognized the virtues of Methodism. Joseph Thaxter, who served as both chaplain and doctor in the battle of Bunker Hill, was also open to other religious options. Methodism gradually found favor among many parishioners across the Vineyard.

Of the various Methodist sites that sprang up across the eastern United States in the nineteenth century, Wesleyan Grove proved to be one of the most prominent and popular camp meetings, with a long heritage and expanding popularity. Today, the gingerbread house–style community of Oak Bluffs is listed in the National Register of Historic Places.

Reformation elder John Adams held a Methodist meeting on West Chop as early as 1827. One of the attendees was the Vineyard's Jeremiah Pease, who became an exhorter, a lay preacher who advocated in place of the minister. It was Jeremiah Pease who selected the Place of Great Trees, as the Native Americans called the site by Squash Meadow Pond that became Wesleyan Grove. When this first revival retreat was held on Martha's Vineyard, committed advocates camped for several days. Preaching was offered thrice daily. Congregants sang hymns by day and prayed by their tents at night.

People who had suffered significant personal loss or sought relief from an upsetting situation found spiritual relief in the Methodist retreat. Revivalism was accepted as a solace for those in need or in pain. Gradually, more and more adherents joined the annual gathering. Many converted to Methodism, which was the intent of the event.

As WORD SPREAD OF the charm of this remote, rustic religious community, throngs of families from various New England parishes joined the annual pilgrimage to the Vineyard. Nine tents were pitched in 1835; more than one hundred filled the oak grove fifteen years later. That number doubled within five years. Over the generations, Wesleyan Grove expanded its network of circular pathways to incorporate tents from all segments in the popular community.

Methodists set the tone for religious retreats, which encouraged more people who were curious about the attraction of the religion. From that blossomed the concept of a vacation getaway, a resort community. Thus was born the tourist of Martha's Vineyard.

The Camp Meeting Association experienced exponential success in a very short time, as additional congregants joined the throngs who gathered for a week of inspirational admonitions from numerous Methodist preachers each summer. More tents were pitched, and more people came. An explosive number of would-be or converted Methodists attended the final Sabbath services each summer.

In 1841, 20 tents arose under the spreading oak trees of Wesleyan Grove, while two thousand people attended the final Sunday of the event. The number of tents doubled the next year and five times that within a decade. In 1853, five thousand people attended the final Sunday service, and six thousand people attended in 1855. By 1858, it was recorded that 320 tents had been pitched and twelve thousand people were in attendance on Sunday. The draw of the Methodist revival community was unrivaled.

Adherents of Wesleyan Grove camped in tents and prayed beneath a canopy of oak trees. Courtesy of the Connie Sanborn collection.

While numerous Methodists who lived on the Vineyard attended Camp Meeting, the majority of attendees were from communities in southeastern Massachusetts and were often sponsored by their local parishes. As more people heard of the annual meeting, parishioners from more disparate towns wanted to participate in the program and journeyed to the Vineyard to partake in its spiritual renewal.

The issue of slavery protruded onto the national stage and the Methodist Church had to deal with it. A schism erupted in 1844 between Southern Methodists who supported slavery and Northerners who favored abolition. From then on, there were two sects of Methodism.

The Vineyard hosted the Camp Meeting Association for a decade, but in 1845, the challenges of access to the island led to a hiatus, and the annual revival meeting was removed to Westport on the southeast coast of Massachusetts. That site was not much easier to reach, and adherents returned to the Vineyard the next year.

Several factors contributed to the growing success of the Camp Meeting Association. Followers praised the healing powers of nature. People believed they received a cure from the saltwater, the communal food and the belief that God's spirit was alive in Wesleyan Grove. The event was reported on and advertised in the Boston press, which expanded the draw and solidified support for the religious revival meeting.

Wesleyan Grove provided an informal, intimate and neighborly community that welcomed families. The morally and physically safe environment created a sense of community that protected children, minimized class distinction and forbid unruly behavior. Unlike the watering places of Saratoga or Newport, Wesleyan Grove was a revival community for the people—the common people. And while the cottages lacked privacy, it was considered a sign of pride to offer the public a view of life in the cottage community.

Participants appreciated the opportunity to share their lives with their children in this religious setting. It kept the children and parents together, strengthening family and neighborly bonds. While religion proved the primary focus of the Wesleyan Grove community, there was also the chance to see and be seen with friends and neighbors without showing off or carrying on with airs of superiority.

"Many cottagers found in Wesleyan Grove a very literal 'home away from home,' populated with acquaintances from home and relatives from other nearby cities, following a social schedule much like that at home, and living in cottages that seemed more like urban parlors than anything else." A sense of rural comfort and casual living conditions prevailed. Wesleyan Grove promoted an informal atmosphere conducive to living a life of community and camaraderie promoted by the culture of the era.[10]

Worshippers pitched tents on platforms arranged in parochial neighborhoods within the thirty-four-acre site. "Circular and radial street patterns were laid out, with Forest Circle established southwest of Trinity Park in 1864 and County Park to the east in 1865. Clinton Avenue boulevard was laid out in 1868." They slept on straw in their tents, ate communally and shared in the spirit of religious revivalism, ignoring the charm of the nearby ocean shores. Congregants pitched their tents outward from the central circle, creating concentric neighborhoods, often of people from the same parish. On occasion, strangers intermingled with a congregation, which led to strangers becoming friends.[11]

With growing numbers of neighbors flocking to the tent city on the shore, friendships and extended social connections forged another bond in the Methodist community. And socialization in the community strengthened over the years. The Vineyard Gazette of 1846, its initial year of publication, remarked how people "seem like one great family, endeared to each other." On occasion, these social aspects proved a stronger bond than the rejuvenation of the religious revival that initially brought the parishioners to the Vineyard.

WHILE THIS FERVENT TENT city flourished and expanded, year after year, more affluent people flocked to fashionable watering places—vacation sites that catered to a more aristocratic crowd. As Vineyard Gazette editor Henry Beetle Hough reported in his 1935 tome devoted to Vineyard tourism, "Before there were summer resorts, there were watering places." These so-called watering places featured mineral springs, a healing balm for invalids, especially in Saratoga, New York. Meanwhile, calming ocean breezes enticed the upper classes to Newport, Rhode Island. Hough included Long Beach and Lake George in this category, while others listed the White Mountains of New Hampshire and the Catskills of New York as popular, expensive vacation retreats.[12]

Those who settled the Wesleyan Grove community were oblivious or chose to ignore the fashionable watering places in other New England sites. The Methodists and their adherents appreciated Wesleyan Grove because it was not an elite site like Saratoga or Newport. These were high-minded religious adherents who refrained from swearing and dancing. They pledged a ministry of minimal pecuniary expense. Methodists reveled in the working class, the poor and those who struggled with adversity. With publicity, promotion, word of mouth and strong religious and social bonds, Wesleyan Grove spread the word of the Vineyard attractions.

And the Vineyard gained recognition as a site with redeeming characteristics, such as the promotion of good health, enjoyment of pleasurable activities and a lifting of spirits. In a historical retrospective of the role of the tourist in 1935, the Vineyard Gazette published an intriguing line describing what the Vineyard afforded the nascent visitor, referencing delightful air, pleasing atmosphere and that "the latter part of the day and evening are the chosen time for the fair to make their appearance."

Again, in the same piece, the Gazette offered additional praise for the charm of the Vineyard, "from its locality, from the fact of its being easy of access, and from the kindness and hospitality of its inhabitants, is one of the finest places of resort in this vicinity." The Gazette also lavished praise on the opportunities for bathing, fishing, sporting activities and the hospitality of the hotels and guest houses that began to spring up in the down-island communities.

In 1858, the Gazette noted sailing and fishing activities along the Vineyard shores, of nature's bounty with cool streams of flowing water, birds chirping

The evolution from tents to cottages was swift. Gingerbread cottages became synonymous with the Methodist Campground. Courtesy of the Connie Sanborn collection.

and flowers blooming. "To Newport wend persons of wealth and fashion," warned the Gazette, though it promoted a visit to the Vineyard, where the "voice of vacation speaks with an urge stronger than ever."

Both steamships and rail service expanded access to Wesleyan Grove, transporting excursionists from far away urban areas to this religious retreat on the sylvan isle.

After twenty years, the environment of Wesleyan Grove evolved. Small, four-room cottages replaced myriad tents beginning in 1857. By the early 1860s, many visitors recognized changes at Wesleyan Grove.

Families who participated in the annual retreat came earlier than camp meeting week to savor the rustic life. Known as rusticators, they emerged as early tourists, seeking a back-to-nature concept, equipped with guidebooks and promotional pamphlets. Thus by the late 1860s, Wesleyan Grove began the transformation from an exclusively religious retreat to a summer resort.

Wesleyan Grove sparked the first full wave of tourists to Martha's Vineyard. The Camp Meeting Association attracted adherents to its Methodist tenets, which drew people to the Vineyard. Many of this first wave of tourists came and saw and went home to spread the word of the rural charm and untouched beauty of the island. Early tourists enjoyed a positive experience and returned each year to savor the friendly, peaceful nature of this island retreat. Others moved to the Vineyard as permanent summer fixtures or year-round residents.

Martha's Vineyard had arrived.

The Camp Meeting Association established a permanent administrative building adjacent to the central oak trees in 1859. The building offered services to the congregants, such as mail delivery, safety regulations, cooperative policies and receiving payments to lease the land. Campground participants came early and stayed later that year. The Grove began to feel like a summer institution.

A Gothic cottage was shipped from Rhode Island in 1859 and erected swiftly and easily. Many more cottages were constructed, gradually replacing the tents. Over the years, additional cottages were built, priced between $150 and $600. Generic features of these four-room cottages included gothic-arched windows, a second-floor balcony with double doors and a front porch. Scrollwork added individual charm to each gingerbread house. Brightly painted trim and adornments improved the allure of every structure. (In many ways, the cottages of the Chautauqua movement that burgeoned across the country in the late nineteenth century mimicked the gingerbread houses of Wesleyan Grove. The Chautauqua adult education program flourished between 1880 and 1920 and, although secular, also offered a communal retreat for adherents.)

Cottages were simply constructed, often of yellow pine secured to the tent platforms. The conventional construction was two rooms downstairs, two rooms upstairs and no kitchen or bathroom. (No kitchen because the Methodists continued to eat communally, and there was fear of fire in the congested development. There was no bathroom because indoor plumbing had not yet been devised.) Because the cottages were designed solely for summer use, there was no effort to insulate or expand the space; sparse was sufficient. Resin from the yellow pine sealed joints between the boards, which resulted in a tight construction for the little houses. Electric lights had not yet been invented; some cottagers purchased candles from Dr. Fisher's spermaceti factory in Edgartown, so candlelight often brightened the campground in the evening.

According to the Massachusetts Historical Commission, "Postwar cottage construction rates intensified, and by 1870, 60 carpenters were employed full-time in the off-season at 'Cottage City.' For the next two decades, the more than 300 tents were gradually replaced by small wooden cottages until more than 500 cottages encompassed the central meeting place of Wesleyan Grove."[13]

For visitors unable to afford or unwilling to build a cottage, the Dunbar House at Montgomery Square by the Arcade opened in 1866 with thirty-one rooms. Renamed the Central House, it expanded to sixty rooms and was later known as Hotel Beatrice. Another hostelry, the Vineyard Grove House on Siloam Street, also accommodated tourists attending the Camp Meeting.

Whether in a tent, cottage, guesthouse or hotel, congregants needed local supplies and services. Local entrepreneurs were more than willing to meet the needs of the tourists and stepped up to the tasks of baking bread, cooking food, cutting hair and washing clothes. A photographer set up shop in the Grove. The Vineyard Gazette published a daily paper, the Camp Meeting Herald, during revival week, highlighting the preachers and events each day. Early on, the residents of Martha's Vineyard saw an opportunity to support the tourist trade and made the most of it.

National newspapers began to take note of the success of the Camp Meeting Association.

As popularity of Wesleyan Grove continued to expand, more cottages were built—the majority between 1857 and 1877. Most cottage owners were shopkeepers and artisans—middle-class businessmen rather than factory workers. Not all cottages were built by tourists or off-islanders; on occasion, Vineyarders built their own cottages and participated in the revival experience.

Over the years, a number of cottages were removed and literally towed away by oxen—some to form double houses and others relocated to another section of the campground or up in the Highlands beyond Lake Anthony.

The Central House, located by the arcade to Wesleyan Grove off Circuit Avenue, was a popular hotel. Courtesy of the Connie Sanborn collection.

Rhode Island governor William Sprague constructed the most expensive structure, Sprague Cottage, for $3,500 in 1869. And the same year, the imposing Crystal Palace of coal magnate Henry Clark was erected across from the current Campground Museum. Six years later, for whatever reason, Clark moved his luxurious structure, including its tower, from the campground to Pequot Avenue a quarter mile away, where it still stands across from Star of the Sea church.

In the midst of this mini housing boom, the Methodists sought a bit of fun and frivolity. Parishioners found delight in knocking wooden balls around the grounds of the Grove, and whenever a free moment arose, before or after Camp Meeting, croquet wickets were staked out. "Croquetting [sic], the great amusement of the rustication season," drew fashionably dressed women and well-attired gentlemen to the game. To the preacher's dismay, croquet advocates occasionally preferred the game to church service. Conflicts arose over who claimed ground for a game. By and large, however, croquet added to the relaxed temperament and brought serene enjoyment to the crowds of Wesleyan Grove.[14]

The Camp Meeting Association bustled, blossomed and bloomed.

Wesleyan Grove patrons set themselves apart from other watering places. "The resort that these industrious and sober citizens made from their camp-meeting grounds reveals a vacationing sensibility far different from that of the educated and fashionable at Newport, Saratoga, and in the mountains." Most cottage owners were strict believers in temperance. Methodist shopkeepers recognized the sins of alcohol and lived their lives accordingly, preaching alcohol abstinence. Importantly, Methodists of the Martha's Vineyard Camp Meeting strongly advocated the national abolition of slavery.[15]

The defining schism of slavery erupted in other Protestant denominations in 1858. The Methodists had split a dozen years earlier over abolition. Now Baptists, Presbyterians, Congregationalists, Episcopalians, Quakers, Catholics and Jews chose to attend the annual Camp Meeting because the Methodists had taken a strong stand in favor of abolition. Members of other denominations wanted to join. Each year, more people attended the annual Camp Meeting in late August.

Change was coming.

In 1860, the Boston Courier noted, "All tourists and excursionists, by sea and land, all romantic young ladies and enterprising young and elderly gentlemen, all journalists and periodical writers, contrive, at some period of a summer, to reach Gay Head." Even today, a century and a half later, a trip to the Gay Head Cliffs is the goal of tourists from far and wide; it is the most dramatic scenic vista on the Vineyard.

Two years later, in 1862, locals were told how to respond to the influx of visitors as they decided "where to choose and where to ramble, and we expect a good many visitors and shall treat them with great cordiality and respect." Massachusetts governor John Andrew visited the Vineyard and addressed a large crowd in 1862, beseeching men to enlist in the Union army. And in 1864, throngs still surged into Wesleyan Grove, "far from the city, out of the workshops, the warerooms, away from domestic cares have come these sojourners in the wilderness to rest awhile." Yes, even during the Civil War, Martha's Vineyard welcomed the summertime tourist crowd.[16]

The Methodist revival meetings held at Wesleyan Grove instigated the tourist industry on Martha's Vineyard.

Even as Wesleyan Grove hosted the governor of Massachusetts, a new population of immigrants gradually made their way to Martha's Vineyard, arriving via the whale ships and sailing vessels that transported people across the Atlantic. This influx of newcomers slowly infiltrated Vineyard life in a peaceful, unobtrusive manner. One may characterize these immigrants as the ultimate tourists, exploring new lands and settling where they could find work and live happily and successfully. And the local people welcomed them. Thus the draw of the whaling economy influenced and impacted the island tourist populace.

3

WHALING IMPACT (1850–1920)

Much has been written about this sea-girt isle.[17]
—The Vineyard as It Was, Is, and Is to Be

When Antone Duarte died in 1931, it was affirmed[18] he was the second Portuguese settler on the Vineyard. He arrived about 1864. Born on Faial Island twenty years earlier, Duarte helped build a small sailing vessel and left the Azores with others, avoiding local military service. After a brief stop in New Bedford, Duarte arrived on Martha's Vineyard. He bought a farm at the head of the Lagoon in Oak Bluffs, and other than a brief visit to Faial in 1910, Duarte spent the next sixty years working the land as a farmer with an off-season job selling ice. He lived with his wife and son Joseph, who inherited his business in 1931. Duarte died at the age of eighty-seven, patriarch to twenty-one grandchildren.

Antone Duart was the ultimate tourist. He came to the Vineyard to seek a new life, found it and made it his own. His life story, and the stories of many others from the Azores and Cape Verdean Islands, represent the powerful attraction of a tourist destination.

The census of Martha's Vineyard in 1850 indicated the population was almost uniformly WASP (white Anglo-Saxon Protestant). A mere fourteen people hailed from overseas and half of those were from the Azores—directly attributed to the whaling industry. The Portuguese influence was small, but in decades to come, especially in the latter part of the nineteenth century, the population grew exponentially.

"There was much more diversity on whaleships. Legend has it that they were the nation's first racially integrated workplaces." Whaleships from New England often docked in the Azores to restock fresh food and drinking water. If the ship needed another sailor, the captain would entice new crew to sign on. After a successful voyage, which might last as long as three years, while unloading barrels of oil in Edgartown, an Azorean crew member occasionally disembarked to make a new home for himself on Martha's Vineyard.[19]

Since the Azores Islands are Portuguese, the new crew spoke a different language. With a dependence on farming and fishing, life in the Azores was similar to that of Martha's Vineyard, which made the transition easier and smoother for these immigrants. Some women journeyed to Martha's Vineyard as well, joining those who had already emigrated from the Azores. And once a few Azoreans were ensconced on the Vineyard, other family members and friends settled there as well.

Soon, a Portuguese community emerged on the Vineyard that continued to welcome the newcomers. Small settlements of immigrants from the Azores and Cape Verdean Islands flourished in parts of Vineyard Haven and Oak

A quarter mile panorama painted in 1848 includes scenes of the Azores, where whaling ships stopped for supplies, water and crew. Courtesy of Thomas Dresser.

Many Azorians discovered a new life on Martha's Vineyard. The environment and lifestyles of the islands were similar. Courtesy of Thomas Dresser.

Bluffs and later in Edgartown, West Tisbury and Chilmark. Portuguese-speaking Azoreans congregated along Lagoon Pond Road in Vineyard Haven and near Wing Road in Oak Bluffs, known as Faial. Vineyard Avenue, in Oak Bluffs, was known as Little Portugal.

Oakland Hall assisted Portuguese immigrants with literacy. Focused on immigrants from the Azores and Cape Verdean Islands, Susan Bradley, the progressive founder, provided literacy training, citizenship education and cultural awareness to the immigrants. When she passed away in 1907, Oscar Denniston, a native of Jamaica, assumed leadership of the mission. He broadened services to include the African American community. Denniston renamed the church Bradley Mission in her honor.

Similarities between the Azores and Martha's Vineyard are of particular interest in the study of tourism and immigration. The climate and landscape of both islands are comparable, which makes it easier for people with an affinity for one environment to adapt naturally into the other.

The islands of the Azores are of a more unique geographical makeup than the Vineyard. The nine islands—São Miguel, Santa Maria, Terceira, Faial, Pico, São Jorge, Graciosa, Flores and Corvo—form a volcanic archipelago nine hundred miles west of Portugal. Living on islands far out to sea provided locals the opportunity to make a living from the sea, which is why Azoreans became proficient fishermen and in demand by the New England whaling industry.

Residents of the Azores immigrated to New England shores, and many made it to Martha's Vineyard. "The more entrepreneurial of them marketed the produce from their gardens and farms, or the fish they brought in from the sea." One family in particular claims a fishmonger ancestor who walked the streets of Oak Bluffs selling fresh-caught halibut, calling out, "alleybut, alleybut." That phrase was shortened to "Alley," a name proudly carried on by the late John Alley (of West Tisbury) and Kerry Alley (of Oak Bluffs) and their respective families. The original fishmonger was Domingo Madeiros or Medeiros. Antone Medeiros, John Alley's ancestor, became a farmer in West Tisbury.[20]

John Alley's father assumed ownership of S.E. Mayhew's General Store in West Tisbury and renamed it Alley's. Other Azorean immigrants opened stores in Oak Bluffs, including Boston Bakery, Oak Bluffs Ice Company on Crystal Lake and Alley Brothers Public Market in Montgomery Square. Local farmers raised pigs and chickens, hence Chicken Alley became a term for Vineyard Avenue. Crops such as potatoes and kale were popular, and flowers like zinnias and marigolds rounded out popular agrarian products for the Portuguese immigrants.

Aside from fishing and farming and operating small shops, newcomers found employment in town services—from teachers to firemen to policemen. They easily adapted to life in a small-town community, built their houses and raised their families.

Perhaps the most prominent immigrant from the Azores to settle on Martha's Vineyard was Joseph A. Sylvia, who represented the Vineyard in the Great and General Court in Boston for thirty years and for whom State Beach is named.

Sylvia's son, Joseph H. Sylvia, failed to return from a bombing mission over Germany in 1944. When his Flying Fortress was hit by enemy fire, he and his crew parachuted from the damaged plane to lighten the load, allowing the pilot to fly the bomber back to England. Sylvia was captured and imprisoned in Germany. He wrote to his father that he was a prisoner of war and was later released.

Other Azoreans are worth considering for their dedicated work ethic as farmers or fishermen. They left the Azores in the last quarter of the nineteenth century and settled on Martha's Vineyard. Their lives exemplify the adventurer who carves a niche in a new land.

Francisco Gularte, anglicized to "Frank Golart," was born in 1839 on the island of Pico. Golart emigrated in 1864 and married in Vineyard Haven. He worked as a mariner and a laborer; two census reports list him as a shoemaker, living on Spring Street in Tisbury. Golart died in 1906.

Mary Maciel was born in Faial and immigrated to New York City in 1899, at the age of twenty. She ventured to Martha's Vineyard about 1905. With her husband, Thomas DeCosta, she lived on North Road in West Tisbury. DeCosta, also from Faial, worked at Seven Gates Farm. Maria Maciel died in 1952.

John Enos Martin was born on Terceira in 1871 and immigrated to New Bedford in 1891. He later made it to Oak Bluffs, living "near the Middle District" of town, which presumably was along Wing Road or Vineyard Avenue. His wife, Mariana Swartz (1870–1938), was also from Terceira and immigrated to Martha's Vineyard in 1892.

Manuel Cabral Mello was born on St. Michael in 1884 and emigrated from the Azores to Boston in 1902. He reached Edgartown a year or so later and worked on a farm for five years before buying

Frank Goulart emigrated from the Azores and settled in Oak Bluffs, an atypical tourist experience. Courtesy of Chris Baer, history.vineyard.net.

a boat and becoming a fisherman. He sailed, fished and shell fished in Vineyard waters for thirty-five years. Captain Mello brought tourists aboard his boat for a day sail. He was a popular figure on the Edgartown waterfront, a prodigious gardener and a true Azorean transplant.

Marion Madeiras (1849–1939) was born in the Azores and immigrated to Oak Bluffs in the mid-1880s. Madeiras bought land along Wing Road, known as Forrest Hill. There he was listed as a farmer in town censuses, residing on Norris Avenue between Vineyard Avenue and Wing Road in the midst of the Portuguese community.

Madeiras married Philomena Fannie Amaral (1849–1939) about 1870. Fannie emigrated from the Azores in 1889. Fannie never spoke English and was illiterate. After her husband's death, Fannie lived on Lagoon Road, surviving to see five generations of descendants.

While the initial reason for relocating from the Azores to Martha's Vineyard may be clouded in history or mystery, descendants of many of the original settlers take pride in learning about and promoting their Azorean heritage. Since the 1920s, the Feast of the Holy Ghost is celebrated on Martha's Vineyard with a parade where celebrants recall their Portuguese heritage and march in traditional attire. The Portuguese American Club in Oak Bluffs is a vibrant community center that welcomes all comers. It is a charitable organization dedicated to support those of Azorian descent.

The Azores have a lot to offer tourists, from markets of lush vegetables and health spas in the hot springs to bicycle rides and beaches. Descendants in the current generation enjoy trips back to the old country to visit the land of their forebears and appreciate the rugged beauty of the homeland.[21]

Local islanders of Azorean descent have traveled to the land of their ancestors and savor a bit of sightseeing as well. John and Anna Alley flew to the Azores in 2010 and visited São Miguel, home of John's grandfather, as well as the islands of Pico, Faial, Terceira and São Jorge. Vineyarder Raymond Moreis Jr. has traveled to the ancient archipelago three times and enjoyed two-week visits. He appreciates the constant sixty-five-degree climate. Dave and Ann Rossi reveled in their trip to the Azores. Pat and Kerry Alley still rave about the thermal heated dinner they savored on a visit to São Miguel.

"The Vineyarders who have made the journey to the mid-Atlantic Azorean islands of their forebears say going once is simply not enough," said tourist author Phyllis Meras. "The sweeping fields, the rocky overlooks above the deep blue sea, the white and black stone cottages on headlands, the mosaic designs of whales and sailing ships that pave the city streets, the seventeenth- and eighteenth-century churches, the hospitable Azoreans—all of it—lure them to journey back."[22]

The Portuguese settled into their Vineyard lifestyle of fishing and farming, as they had in the Azores. Immigrants from the Azores appreciated the opportunity to settle on the Vineyard just as the Methodists appreciated the opportunity to pray there. Yet all was not well with the patrons of Wesleyan Grove as the decade of the 1860s drew to a close.

The Camp Meeting Association faced a new risk on the perimeter of the Grove—a challenge in its audacity and intrusion to the religious purview of the Methodist community. This activity threatened to disrupt the placid patrons of the Grove. Yet it proved a symbiotic injection of enthusiasm and involvement in the Vineyard community.

4

FIRST TOURIST WAVE (1865–80)

Thatplacebeingthegrandcentreofattractionandinterestforthewholeisland.[23]
—Tourist Guide of Cottage City

T he patrons of Wesleyan Grove wanted to pray in peace and explore the Vineyard as tourists, yet they felt thwarted and threatened by the plans of a newcomer to the island.

Promoter and businessman Erastus Carpenter of Foxboro Massachusetts camped in a tent at Wesleyan Grove more than once. He liked the experience so much that he decided to build a house in the campground. However, because the campground owns the land, he would have to pay a lease. That was his impetus to build nearby.

Because Carpenter wanted to share the experience of living on Martha's Vineyard, he made it happen on his terms. He considered the land adjacent to the campground idyllic as well and thought "such a place should be enjoyed by more than those God-fearing Methodists who came for a few days of praying in August." He anticipated developing the shoreline into a summer resort community.[24]

Sufficient money was available to purchase property because, as the whaling industry continued to fade, money that had been invested in whale ships was available for other options, such as land development. Local captain Shubael Lyman Norton and four other investors met with Carpenter to create a planned community of summer houses for people to enjoy vacation or summertime on Martha's Vineyard.

Erastus Carpenter organized the Oak Bluffs Land & Wharf Company to develop land just east and adjacent to Wesleyan Grove. His development, laid out in 1866, was the first planned community in the country—three years ahead of landscape architect Frederick Law Olmsted's village of Riverside, Illinois.

Shubael Norton invested much of his seventy-five acres of local land in this commercial enterprise and became an active partner in the project. He determined that by dividing the acreage into house lots, he could encourage tourists to invest in a small piece of this potential resort community. One thousand lots were put on the market for eager customers to purchase and build houses. Norton and his wife built a house for themselves in Hartford Park.

The six men who formed the Oak Bluffs Land & Wharf Company held a common principle: "All of these men were visionaries, men of ego and ambition for whom failure wasn't a consideration. These were leaders who were accustomed to using their social and political appetites to meet their personal goals." By working together, they developed a successful enterprise that flourished for years.[25]

Carpenter constructed a wharf that extended out into Vineyard Sound in 1866. This provided steamship access to his new development, as well as to the Camp Meeting Association.

Shubael Norton sold much of his farmland to the Oak Bluffs Land & Wharf Company, creating the site that became a summer resort. Courtesy of Joyce Dresser.

That same year, landscape architect Robert Morris Copeland, a peer of Frederick Law Olmstead, was hired to design a massive planned residential community. "Copeland took the circular motif of Wesleyan Grove and expanded it into an elaborately curved, studiedly informal design mirroring the intimacy of scale at Wesleyan Grove, but maintaining more normal spatial arrangements." Copeland had designed cemeteries, and his plan for Oak Bluffs, modified a couple of times, created a cohesive seaside community that was welcoming and unique, with numerous parks scattered about.[26]

The Copeland plan had reason to mimic the campground with winding roadways and avenues, ocean views and numerous small parks. Carpenter wanted his development to mirror Wesleyan Grove to be a cooperative element rather than a competitive distraction. Copeland designed a grand loop around the community, known as the Circuit. Reviewing maps of the era, it is clear that Circuit Avenue was designed to circumscribe the land development project of the Oak Bluffs Land & Wharf Company, which featured the picturesque park along the waterfront, welcoming tourists off the steamers.

Ocean Park was intended to be the impressive first sight that greeted visitors to the Vineyard. It was. And "today, arriving on a ferry, Oak Bluffs framed by Ocean Park is the picture visitors see in their mind's eye when they think of Martha's Vineyard, the iconic scene created by the passion of the Captains of Cottage City."[27]

At the time, right after the Civil War, the area was still part of the town of Edgartown. There were rumblings that the townspeople in Edgartown proper wanted to benefit from the numerous tourists visiting Wesleyan Grove. And there were worries that this new development would impinge on the Edgartown tax base by requiring more town services.

Carpenter began to sell house lots in this area he called Oak Bluffs. His flyer on July 5, 1867, was the first time the name Oak Bluffs was used publicly. Carpenter sold the choicest lots around Ocean Park to prominent prospective customers: physician Harrison Tucker, hardware magnate Philip Corbin, toolmaker Timothy Stanley. These individuals promised to erect impressive structures, adding to the dramatic welcoming scene for tourists arriving aboard steamships that docked by Ocean Park. Erastus Carpenter built his own imposing house on Ocean Park as well.

Nearby, leaders of Wesleyan Grove feared the impending challenges of commercial influence and interference by the Oak Bluffs Land & Wharf Company. In 1866, "a whole new set of challenges to the religious purity of Wesleyan Grove [appeared] in that year. The pursuit of profit, even more than the pursuit of pleasure, seemed to threaten the purposes of Wesleyan Grove."[28]

Initially, there was contention between the two groups. From August 1866 through April 1867, the Methodists feared the encroaching commercial enterprise. Whether to curtail curious non-Methodists from impinging on campground sermons or restrict Methodists from imbibing or frequenting the forbidden pleasures of Circuit Avenue, a seven-foot wooden stockade fence was erected around the thirty-four-acre site of the Camp Meeting Association in 1867. The gate was locked at 10:00 p.m., but wily Methodists found loose slats they could wiggle through when they missed the curfew. The fence was in place only a short time, while the campground struggled with its new neighbors, the Oak Bluffs Land & Wharf Company. (We have been unable to locate any photos of the fence.)

The Camp Meeting Association purchased additional acreage across Squash Meadow Pond in the nearby Vineyard Highlands as a protective buffer should they feel the need to relocate. This land purchase was proposed and funded by an offshoot organization, the Vineyard Grove Company.

Instead of posing a threat to the Methodist meeting, the Oak Bluffs Land & Wharf Company sought to work cooperatively with Wesleyan Grove. Rather than competing or opposing Wesleyan Grove, Oak Bluffs Land & Wharf embraced it and built on it. Its initial map of the development expanded on the campground model.

Both groups encountered challenges in balancing the strengths and differences between the religious and secular perspectives. The leaders of Wesleyan Grove faced a difficulty in sustaining a community that welcomed the less-wealthy Methodist revivalists. The leaders of Oak Bluffs encouraged relatively well-off cottagers who sought tourist options rather than the providence offered by religious saviors. The two communities sought to overlap their ideals and services and managed to do so for the most part.

The directors of the new company realized the religious community could support and promote its own development plans; the Methodist revivalists could appreciate and encourage the growth of Oak Bluffs as a resort community. Instead of competing, the two operations could and did develop a symbiotic relationship.

Erastus Carpenter seized on a novel concept as he set about his development under the auspices of the Oak Bluffs Land & Wharf Company.

He advocated the heretofore unknown belief that working men and women deserved a break in their routine of labor by savoring a vacation. This idea filtered down to the middle class. Vacationing became a legitimate activity; time spent in leisure pursuits came to be recognized as a valuable asset to healthy living.

Island historian Skip Finley observed, "Early Oak Bluffs blossomed, its growth geometric as middle-class people from Massachusetts and other parts of the Northeast discovered the pleasant new seaside watering place with its wonderful summer climate and quaint, picturesque homes." The birth of the middle class in the late nineteenth century proved a boon to the nascent resort community founded on the shores of Martha's Vineyard.[29]

The new community set itself apart as the directors moved expeditiously to promote the opportunity to purchase property near the ocean shore. Oak Bluffs was explicitly advertised as less expensive than aristocratic Newport or Saratoga Springs. It was intended for those who desired to spend time along the beaches and shoreline, appreciating the benefits gleaned from the sea air, foregoing the restrictive standards and arrogant airs of more fashionable, crowded and expensive watering places. Oak Bluffs was designed to be a unique summer resort that was affordable for the middle class and idyllic in its seaside atmosphere.

The expanded development of the Oak Bluffs Company proved mutually beneficial to Wesleyan Grove—each community benefited from the other.

Nevertheless, separate wharfs for the competing groups of patrons were constructed in the late 1860s. Highland Pier was built for the Methodists adjacent to the present East Chop Beach Club in 1869. The Town Pier at the present Steamship Wharf was rebuilt in 1872. By 1869, the Oak Bluffs Land & Wharf Company could boast a primitive hotel, fire engines, the wharf and success in selling off most of its inventory of one thousand house lots.

The more prominent people of Oak Bluffs built cottages that dominated the landscape in the early years. Dr. Harrison Tucker's summer cottage on Ocean Park, built in 1870, cost $11,000 and was most decorative. He illuminated his domicile with thirty gas-fed lights. As the patent medicine man, Tucker earned rapport with the rich and famous, hosting President Ulysses Grant in August 1874, to view a grand fireworks display.

Founder Erastus Carpenter built his summer abode, also on Ocean Park, for $12,000 in 1868. As a promotional device, Carpenter conceived Illumination Night, established initially for his Oak Bluffs Land & Wharf Company community. The grand illumination was Carpenter's effort to

Dr. Harrison Tucker built an imposing structure on the edge of Ocean Park. Courtesy of the Connie Sanborn collection.

The house of Erastus Carpenter, founder of the Oak Bluffs Land & Wharf Company, stands proudly on Ocean Park. Courtesy of Joyce Dresser.

draw visitors to the Ocean Park area, and he was unashamed to request owners of the first few cottages to hang lanterns on their porches. In 1869, Illumination Night expanded to include Wesleyan Grove in the celebration. The Camp Meeting Association has celebrated Illumination Night ever since.

Houses designed and sold to tourists or adventurers by the Oak Bluffs Land & Wharf Company assumed picturesque characteristics similar to those of Wesleyan Grove. The new cottages mimicked with elaborate design and gothic windows and often included double doors upstairs. (The doors served a double duty, as furniture could be hoisted up through the doorway because the stairs were narrow.) Two significant differences were that the Oak Bluffs houses were often more spacious because they were set on larger lots, and many enjoyed a partial view of the ocean. The houses were built in various styles, primarily Queen Anne, which proved an eclectic mix of design and décor. Carpenter promoted cottages with Mansard roofs, towers and turrets, often more dramatic than the campground cottages. This style is called New England Carpenter Gothic in his honor.

The melding of the two communities was deemed a success. "And it also acted to broaden the appeal of the two places taken together, by expanding

The Oak Bluffs House welcomed the New York Yacht Club. The observation tower looms to the left of this Victorian structure. Courtesy of the Martha's Vineyard Museum.

the ways in which they could include the secular and the sacred, the profit-making and the pleasure-seeking, in one place."

As Dona Brown writes, "By the end of the 1860s, the development of Oak Bluffs had substantially changed the nature of what was now being referred to as 'Cottage City,' not by eliminating or directly competing with the religious atmosphere at Wesleyan Grove, but by expanding the range of possibilities while maintaining the sense of religious safety."[30]

Tourists kept coming, whether to partake in the Wesleyan Grove religious experience or the secular vacation atmosphere offered by the Oak Bluffs Land & Wharf Company. "The community was growing in the 1870s with new real estate developments and an increasing number of visitors, summer residents and permanent year-round residents."[31]

The appeal of the summer resort community was heralded far afield. Each year brought more tourists to the Vineyard. Steamship service accommodated the influx with as many as twenty boats a day docking at the wharves of Oak Bluffs, bringing thousands of day-trippers from southeastern Massachusetts to partake in the resort experience. Hotel guests and cottage owners added to the crowds of daily excursionists.

In 1877, the Gazette referenced the medicinal benefits of the Vineyard in a promotional review of the island's pristine, pure atmosphere. "The climate during the sultry summer season is deliciously cool and invigorating, being tempered by the ameliorating influences of the neighboring Gulf Stream." And without a doubt, the beauty of the Gay Head Cliffs was etched in the tourist's memory with clay of "red, blue, white, yellow and green, all blended together in motley unison." This review was written long before the dramatic clay colors faded and much of the imposing landscape eroded into Vineyard Sound.

A popular activity for Oak Bluffs tourists in this era was a carriage ride out to West Tisbury, which was half as far as Gay Head and had a very different sight to see. Gazette editor Henry Beetle Hough noted that "excursionists came flocking" from the down-island Vineyard shores to visit Nancy Luce, a spinster iconoclast, who lived with her hens in the rustic setting of New Lane in West Tisbury. Horse-drawn carriages journeyed from Oak Bluffs through Holmes Hole to West Tisbury. The woman of the hens or the "Laureate of Hens," as noted by the Atlantic Monthly, was a unique tourist attraction. Nancy Luce sold photos of herself and her hens, as well as books of her poetry. She was an effective, efficient entrepreneur—an outcast yet willing to take money from curious tourists. Her house became a point of destination, and even today, her grave at the West Tisbury cemetery at Dead Man's Curve on State Road is festooned with plaster chickens left by curious tourists of another generation.

As the influx of tourists grew year by year, Vineyard Haven and Edgartown were listed as "these two Elysiums," combining seashore and country landscapes to entice the weary denizen of the urban area. The Vineyard proved a delight with "snug, compact villages," hosting hotels to meet the tourist's needs and providing "the freedom and opportunities for recreation afforded by the unlimited 'sea-room' and the close proximity of forest and field." In short, the Vineyard offered a natural environment well suited to offer a vacation to the hard-working city dweller.

As the Oak Bluffs Land & Wharf Company sold the last of its one thousand house lots, the income flow dropped, but the costs of operating a planned community rose. Streets needed maintenance, grounds required care and the upkeep of wharves and landscaping was too much for the company to handle. The town of Edgartown refused to pay these expenses, which became an incentive for residents and businesses of Oak Bluffs to secede from Edgartown.

The majority of the board of directors decided to sell off the Oak Bluffs town parks to raise additional funds. Erastus Carpenter claimed the parks belonged to the community; nevertheless, his fellow directors still voted to sell. Boston attorney George Abbott paid $7,500 for the parks but was challenged in court. He won the first round but lost on appeal to Justice Oliver Wendell Holmes Jr., and the parks were conveyed back to the town in perpetuity. This was considered a victory for the general populace as it prevented further development on the greenswards of the community. The nine original Oak Bluffs parks are Ocean, Hartford, Waban, Penacook, Niantic, Hiawatha, Naushon, Nashawena and Petaluma. Viera Park should be included in this enumeration

Tourism flourished in the latter half of the nineteenth century. Cottage City was recognized as part of a movement to provide a vacation getaway, an escape, for different social classes. It was not a high-brow watering place but a summer resort for the common man. The majority of tourists were enamored of Oak Bluffs. "It was not Eden to everyone, but for better or worse Cottage City still offered an image of leisure shorn of its aristocratic and extravagant associations, one which instead associated

The Sea View House bustled with activity in downtown Cottage City until it was destroyed by a suspicious fire in 1892. Courtesy of the Martha's Vineyard Museum.

leisure with an unpretentious style, family intimacy, and the Christian duty of relaxation."[32]

The line between the secular resort community and oak-shaded religious retreat was blurred as adherents of both persuasions were drawn to the seaside site on the shores of Lake Anthony. Once the stockade fence between the two sections of town was removed, the communities overlapped and expanded to welcome all comers.

Erastus Carpenter continued to promote and expand his development of Oak Bluffs. To accommodate those tourists who did not build a cottage or house in either community, hotels were constructed in the downtown area, primarily along Circuit Avenue near the steamship wharf, providing easy access for tourists.

Excursionists enjoyed hotels, which proved a necessity for many people of the era. The Pawnee, Metropolitan and Island House flourished on Circuit Avenue along the edge of the campground. The Island House, built in 1872, was the sole year-round hotel. In 1909, it was the only hotel with a liquor license in southeastern Massachusetts. The lower level of the Island House is extant today, adjacent to Murdick's Fudge on Circuit Avenue.

The most elegant hotel was the Sea View House, which opened on July 23, 1872, featuring the first passenger elevator on the Vineyard, speaking tubes for communication, gas lights and steam heat. The Sea View cost $100,000 to build. It featured a dramatic structure with twin turrets that impressed island visitors from afar. The 125 rooms were in great demand. And it even had a few indoor bathrooms—a decided luxury in an era when indoor plumbing was virtually unknown.

The Wesley House, built in 1880, housed a curio shop with clay tchotchkes from Gay Head. Today, the Wesley is the only original Cottage City hotel still operating as a hotel. It survives as Summercamp, still welcoming tourists to its rooms that now overlook Oak Bluffs harbor. When Lake Anthony was opened to the ocean in 1900, the harbor of Oak Bluffs was formed, and the front of the Wesley was focused away from the campground to face the harbor.

"Hotels like the Sea View in many ways came to represent the seaside resort in the public imagination. Even today, seventy-five years after most of them burned down, the 'great hotels' remain foremost in the public imagination of late nineteenth century vacationing." At the height of the tourist expansion era prior to 1900, eighteen hotels sought to meet the needs of the expansive number of visitors to Cottage City.[33]

OAK BLUFFS WAS PROMOTED as the "Great American Watering Place," akin to Long Branch, New Jersey; Saratoga Springs; or Newport. Two unique aspects of this summer resort were the concept of "bluffing," which was a romantic evening stroll where a couple would casually walk arm in arm along the seaside boardwalk that stretched more than half a mile along the shore. And the dance hall upstairs at the Tivoli on the site of the current police station housed a summer dance band that played for decades and featured songs like "The Oak Bluffs Galope" and "Tivoli Girl."

WHILE THE HOTEL GUESTS and homeowners of Oak Bluffs danced and pranced along the seashore, patrons of Wesleyan Grove continued to flock to their preachers and worship each August.

The trees in the ancient oak grove were aging and no longer providing sufficient canopy for the religious services. In 1870, the last of the oaks were cut down. In their place, an immense canvas tabernacle was stitched together, erected and stretched across tall poles to replace the oak trees. This massive tent incorporated four thousand yards of sailcloth and weighed one ton. For nearly a decade, this canvas canopy was erected each spring and taken down at the end of the summer. The canvas tabernacle provided a central gathering canopy until 1879, with construction of the wrought-iron tabernacle, which arched over the Camp Meetings and is still in use today. Now tourists and locals share an open-air meeting place, which seats three thousand. (The original benches were refinished and repaired by Robert Gatchell in 2017.)

In the waning years of the nineteenth century, the Methodists considered their haven unlike the popular aristocratic watering places of Newport and Saratoga Springs. Besides their religious services, Methodists played endless games of croquet in the campground. Sunbathing oftentimes replaced Bible worship. Religious conversions to Methodism slacked off year by year. Methodism still dominated the culture, but there was a decided relaxation of the strict concepts of the early days of the Camp Meeting program.

The tabernacle stands as the religious and social focal point of the campground community. Courtesy of Joyce Dresser.

This postcard of the tabernacle represents the focal point of religious and secular community on the Vineyard. Courtesy of the Martha's Vineyard Museum.

Hebron Vincent, who documented the history of Wesleyan Grove from 1835 to 1869, offered a rebuttal to those who feared that the congregants had strayed from their esteemed goals. He argued that at least Wesleyan Grove provided religion, as well as leisure activities, whereas Saratoga Springs and Newport were simply places to squander money. As Methodism came to grips with the newly minted values of leisure time and relaxation for the middle class, the clergy had to acknowledge that rest and relaxation could be compatible with religion.

The melding of religious services and resort relaxation in the two communities worked brilliantly. The Oak Bluffs Land & Wharf Company built on and co-opted and morphed with Wesleyan Grove to create Cottage City. Cottage City became known as a less prestigious, less expensive but more popular summer resort than Saratoga or Newport.

Of all the excitement and activity aroused by these two summer enclaves, one historian properly assessed the status of the nascent resort community: "These years were perhaps the most frenzied in Vineyard history." A good deal of activity was underway, centered primarily in Oak Bluffs but expanding out and across the rest of the island.[34]

An 1871 issue of the Whaleman's Shipping List noted the influx of traffic to the Vineyard: "Ho for the Vineyard! A large stream of travel is now rushing through this city [New Bedford] to the Vineyard. Every conceivable kind of vehicle groans with its freight of humanity; men and women of all nations and all natures, of all sections and complexions—the Portuguese, the Englishman, the Frenchman, the Southerner, the Easterner—all going to the Eden-like city by the sea."

The Vineyard had arrived as a vacation destination.

5

LAND DEVELOPMENT (1870–1910)

Martha's Vineyard: Isle of Dreams and Health.[35]

E rastus Carpenter had such success with his Oak Bluffs Land & Wharf Company that he wanted to replicate it in another part of the island.

And numerous land developers and speculators were inspired to invest in the creation of similar resort communities down-island. The economic opportunities afforded by the development of a tourist settlement led to numerous business propositions, some with more positive results than others. More than two thousand acres were appropriated by various developments, principally in Oak Bluffs but also Vineyard Haven and Edgartown. The up-island landscape remained unscathed in this era.

By one calculation, the majority of land development projects that followed went out of business or bankrupt in the Panic of 1873. The Oak Bluffs Land & Wharf Company was unique in its stability. Erastus Carpenter was enchanted by his initial project and determined to expand his dream and develop a second site on Martha's Vineyard.

Carpenter planned his new development in another section of Edgartown. This project would be far removed from steamship service and the Methodist campground; however, the attraction of a hotel and house lots along the shore was too persuasive for Carpenter, and he went to work to develop this new community in Katama, the open grasslands south of Edgartown.

This vast open area was ripe for construction, at least in Carpenter's mind. His initial plan included steamships ferrying guests through Edgartown Harbor to his hotel on Katama Bay. When that proved problematic,

Erastus Carpenter planned a second resort community in Katama. The Mattakesett Lodge was to be the centerpiece. Courtesy of the Connie Sanborn collection.

Carpenter promoted the Martha's Vineyard Railroad. The railroad could be an ideal means to transport tourists from Oak Bluffs to Katama. (Later, a spur to South Beach was added, where the dramatic surf, cool breezes and scenic sights would entice the curious, the adventurous and the naturalist.)

Again, Carpenter hired Robert Morris Copeland to design his planned community with winding roadways and plenty of parkland. Carpenter hoped his development would succeed near the appealing surf of South Beach and not too far from the excitement of the county seat of Edgartown. (A primary feature lacking in Katama was the draw of the Methodist campground that had inspired and encouraged development in Oak Bluffs.)

THE MATTAKESET LODGE WAS to be bigger and better than the Sea View House in Oak Bluffs. Under the moniker Katama Land Company, and spearheaded by retired whaling captain Nathan Jernegan, the Mattakeset opened for business in August 1873. While intended to be a gatehouse to a grander hotel, the Mattakeset Lodge was the only hotel built in Katama. House lots were diligently plotted across the landscape, but none were purchased or built on. Only a few people ventured out to Katama during the first year the hotel was in operation. The Lodge was not financially feasible during this first year.

It was not until a year later, on August 17, 1874, that the Martha's Vineyard Railroad reached the lodge, and paying customers enjoyed luxurious accommodations near the surf of South Beach but far from the bustle of Edgartown. The Mattakeset Lodge remained open beyond the time the railroad stopped operations in the late 1890s. The lodge closed its doors in 1905. (Two sections of the lodge were removed to Edgartown proper—one installed at the Harbor View Hotel and the other as the Land Bank headquarters by Cannonball Park.)

The website of the Winnetu Oceanside Resort, the current hotel in the area, observes, "To accommodate the demands of its day, a narrow-gauge railroad was built, connecting the Oak Bluffs Steamship Wharf (same location as today) with Edgartown—out to Katama and the Mattakeset Lodge and South Beach. The South Beach rail stop was at the same site as today's Winnetu Hotel."

The Martha's Vineyard Railroad opened for service in August 1874. The train picked up passengers from the ferry in Oak Bluffs and transported them through Edgartown and on to Katama. This brought more tourists to Edgartown; their spending was intended to partially replace the dollars lost in the declining whaling industry. Passenger service peaked in 1882 with 21,142 passengers, but the railroad never made money.

One of the more unique features of the Mattakeset Lodge was its location. Besides the sumptuous accommodations, the hotel took advantage of the cool sea breezes that blew across South Beach in the summer. Picnics, clambakes and dances were all the rage, and the lodge soon earned a reputation as a hospitable haven for excursionists.

The luxurious Lodge depended on the railroad, yet there was negligible interest by tourists for the house lots in Katama. The Martha's Vineyard Railroad never turned a profit, partially due to low ridership, but also because annual maintenance expenses were devoted to track repair along State Beach. Sand did not provide a firm base to lay the track.

More tourists did reach Edgartown in the years the railroad ran. And with more tourists, there was a need for more guest accommodations. That led to construction of the Harbor View Hotel in 1891, located on Starbuck Neck overlooking the lighthouse on the harbor, nearly a mile from the train station at the current Depot Corner. (The hotel went bankrupt within a year but soon regained its footing and today is solvent and key to the tourist trade of Edgartown.) The name Harbor View was suggested by Leonard Bliss of Regal Shoe, who is said to have driven the first automobile on the Vineyard. The hotel opening drew four hundred guests.

THE VISIT FROM PRESIDENT Ulysses S. Grant coincided with the opening of the railroad. This first visit by a sitting United States president and Civil War hero put the Vineyard on the map as an esteemed vacation destination. And it thrust Oak Bluffs into the forefront of the sites that tourists craved to visit and enjoy. Grant's visit further cemented the unity between the Methodist community and the secular Oak Bluffs Land & Wharf operation. Without intent, Grant single-handedly assured that Martha's Vineyard gained prominence as a must-see tourist destination.

Grant's visit has long been touted as the onset of the resort establishment and tourist community of Martha's Vineyard. That statement stands the test of time. The eighteenth president's three-day visit is still cited as having made an enduring impact on the Vineyard. Nearly a century and a half later, we acknowledge the influence of Grant's visit, although it was brief and he spent as much time visiting Nantucket and the Cape as he did Cottage City.

President Grant's visit to Wesleyan Grove in 1874 had a major impact on the rise of tourism on Martha's Vineyard. Courtesy of the Connie Sanborn collection.

THE TOWNSPEOPLE OF THE section of Edgartown that included Oak Bluffs had talked of secession for more than a decade. Divergent goals of the two communities split the town of Edgartown. The town proper, surrounding Edgartown Harbor, sought to replace income lost in the whaling industry with a new economic engine: the tourist trade of Oak Bluffs. Residents of the western section of Edgartown, which encompassed the Methodist campground and the Oak Bluffs Land & Wharf Company, felt they were not fairly treated by Edgartown proper.

Tax monies were not used where the western segment of the town needed them, specifically the road along State Beach and the Lagoon Bridge to Vineyard Haven. Beach Road, along what became State Beach, was merely a dirt road when it was constructed and opened in January 1872. It became known as the cheesecloth highway in 1895, when the roadway was rebuilt, using cheesecloth to secure the moving sand. Lagoon Bridge was built in March 1871 and caused friction with Edgartown because the town fathers saw no financial gain to be realized.

Howes Norris, son of the captain slain in the Sharon whaleship mutiny of 1842 and editor of the Cottage City Star, was a prime mover in the secession of Cottage City from Edgartown. The movement was organized by and for the tourist segment to withdraw from Edgartown proper and establish a new town. Norris had a pier on the shores of Vineyard Haven harbor that was used by Camp Meeting adherents before construction of the piers in Eastville and the Highlands. (Remnants of Norris's landing form an outcropping across from the current hospital.)

Norris gained sufficient votes in the town meeting of 1880, and a new town was created. Before the final name was chosen, other options under discussion included Bonaire, Marthasburg, Oak Bluffs and the Cottage City of America. The final decision was to name the new town Cottage City. (In 1907, Cottage City was renamed Oak Bluffs.) Edgartown proper lost a significant tax base, and the tourist town was now on its own.

(To expand the discussion on local town divisions, Chilmark separated from its southern section in 1871, creating the town of Gay Head, renamed Aquinnah in 1998. In 1892, the southwest section of Tisbury broke away, creating the town of West Tisbury. While neither of these latter divisions could be directly attributed to the rise of tourism or increase in population, the additional towns did reflect the expanding sectional separation the Vineyard encountered and addressed in the latter quarter of the nineteenth century.)

In 1869, with the intent to improve navigation along Vineyard Sound, Captain Silas Daggett, who lived on East Chop Drive along the bluffs of Oak Bluffs, built the East Chop lighthouse, known as the Coaster's Light. Two years later, he added telegraph service across the sound to Falmouth. The government built the present lighthouse in 1876, which still sits atop Telegraph Hill—a beacon for passing maritime traffic.

To expand tourist business on the Vineyard, Erastus Carpenter and Edgartown's wealthy entrepreneur Daniel Fisher encouraged the extension of Old Colony Railroad from Wareham to Woods Hole, which occurred in 1872. That spur led to expanded steamship service from Woods Hole to the Vineyard and the concurrent increase in tourists visiting the Vineyard. Consequently, New Bedford lost a key service for its port, even as the whaling industry crumbled, which proved a double financial impact to the Whaling City.

With the increase in tourism, there was a rise in the number of sites where tourists could buy property and become regular seasonal visitors. This was the motivating factor in many of the prospective land development projects.

The increase in tourists prompted developers to offer what people wanted: to partake in the unique charms of the island community. Numerous land development schemes got underway, some with moderate success, while others quickly folded in bankruptcy or disinterest. The underlying goal of each development was to entice more tourists to travel to the Vineyard, put down their money and purchase a piece of the rock. Someone would make a financial windfall from it if all went according to plan.

The Methodists had taken a protective step in 1869, when they purchased land in the Highlands north of Squash Meadow Pond. This site, known as Vineyard Grove, was to serve as an escape hatch should the anticipated encroachment by the Oak Bluffs Land & Wharf Company be too harsh for the Methodist enclave to bear.

By 1875, the Methodists no longer feared competition from Carpenter's company, so they sold the land to a Baptist group. The Baptists renamed their site Wayland Grove and formed a religious revival community similar to Wesleyan Grove. The New England Black Baptist Association settled there in summers. Highland Wharf by the present East Chop Beach Club became known as the Baptist Landing.

Squash Meadow Pond originally extended all the way to School Street. A bulkhead or bridge was built across the pond in 1869, which created Sunset

Lake. This bridge served as a link between the two religious retreats—the Baptists and the Methodists—and was known as crossing the River Jordan. At one time, the plank walkway along the bulkhead by Sunset Lake was considered as a park called Lakeview, but that plan fell by the wayside.

The new pond was called Lake Anthony and proved popular in downtown Cottage City. It was dredged, and a cut made through to the ocean in 1900, creating the harbor of Oak Bluffs. Opening Lake Anthony solved two problems: elimination of the pollution in the pond and welcoming oceangoing craft into the newly created harbor.

A large octagonal wooden Baptist tabernacle was built at Wayland Grove in the Highlands and opened for services in August 1878. It seated two thousand people. In 1881, the Baptist community added Illumination Night to its grove, marking the third community to participate in this annual celebration of the end of summer.

After many years of service, the Baptist tabernacle fell into disuse and disrepair around 1930. The building burned in a suspicious fire in 1944. Today, the circle in the Highlands has a pair of pathways running through the overgrown area with concrete foundations poking through the grass. The Highlands exists as a homogeneous community to this day.

At one time, part of this area served as a sprawling sheep pasture, and over the years, it became a golf course. Still later, now tree-covered, part of this landscape evolved into the East Chop Tennis Club.

Paddle boats were a familiar sight on Lake Anthony before it was opened to the ocean. The "W" of the Wesley Hotel is in the background. Courtesy of the Martha's Vineyard Museum.

The Martha's Vineyard Summer Institute on the shores of Vineyard Sound was the first summer school intended to teach teachers how to teach. The school opened sixteen classrooms in 1880. Courses were offered in elocution, language, literature, shorthand and the arts and sciences. More than 1,500 students attended summer classes between 1880 and 1907. Gradually, other colleges assumed the role of teacher education and the Summer Institute closed its doors.

Numerous land development projects were proposed across the island as land speculation gained a substantial audience. While this list is incomplete, it indicates a number of the planned communities:

Bay View (a 6-acre development)
Bellevue Heights (surrounded Crystal Lake on East Chop)
Cedar Neck
Central Place (12 acres)
Engleside
Forest Hills (about 20 acres)
Lagoon Heights and Grovedale (300 acres)
Oak Point
Ocean (8 acres)
Ocean Heights no. 1 (between Farm Pond and Sengiekontacket)
Ocean Heights no. 2 (laid out by a Scotsman named Laidlaw along the Edgartown–Vineyard Haven Road and Sengekontacket with the numbered streets. It is a viable development today.)
Ocean View and Lookout Mountain (75 acres near Trapp's Pond in Edgartown. The slightly elevated landscape gave rise to the name.)
Oklahoma, where Innisfail was developed (150 acres)
Prospect and Sea View (each 15 acres)
Sunset
Vineyard Highlands, also known as Wayland Grove (225 acres around the Baptist tabernacle)
West Point Grove (about 40 acres on West Chop)

In 1880, the Gazette praised the opening of a new, unnamed hotel with first class appointments. The atmosphere was great for those tourists who liked to sail, fish or bathe. The hotel offered free carriage rides to and from the ferry. This was probably the Prospect House in Lagoon Heights. When the trolley line was extended up Wing Road onto Alpine, linking the area to downtown Cottage City, Lagoon Heights became a development, with the Prospect House as the anchor of the community. The proprietors of Lagoon Heights built a wharf that snaked into the water for sailboats and swimming. Two New Bedford whalemen, the Wing brothers, ran Lagoon Heights, hence nearby Wing Road.

The Prospect House was built off Alpine Avenue in 1874. It boasted twenty-two rooms and a cupola to scan the landscape. The natural wonders of the Vineyard promoted a convincing argument. In an 1880 tourist guide, Prospect House advertised that it "offers superior attractions as a summer resort," and "its appointments are, in every sense of the word, first class." The advertisement boasted croquet groves, extensive forests and "pure water, filtered by sand, and noted far and wide for its medicinal properties, renders this the most healthful and invigorating resort in America." According to this promotion, the Vineyard joined the ranks of prestigious watering places in the Northeast.

The Prospect House burned in 1898. Today, the development is a conglomeration of house styles in a rustic setting.

The Oklahoma settlement, also along the lagoon, had an awkward beginning, a flourishing mid-life and too soon was virtually extinct. Howes Norris purchased land on the Edgartown–Vineyard Haven Road in 1872. The property was later the site for a grand hotel perched on the edge of the lagoon, and a massive development project was designed along the shores. In the 1870s, the land was treeless and open but also remote and without adequate means of access, except a long walk or horseback ride along a dusty roadway from downtown Vineyard Haven. Prospective property purchasers were advised to reach the area by steamer from across the lagoon.

An impressive hotel, Innisfail, was built on the land that was to be the centerpiece of Oklahoma. The word innisfail means a place of peace and rest, and to that end, it served its name well. Innisfail became a resort for musicians and singers—a haven of fellowship and song. Irishman Tom Karl sang light opera, and Dellon Dewey was his avid promoter and sidekick. Innisfail musicians performed concerts for visitors and guests into the early 1890s.

Plans were made for dozens of cottages in the Oklahoma development, but the project was never developed due to the fragile financial economy and limited access. Only three small cottages were built; they are still extant. One cottage houses a mural painted along an upper wall of one room, which offers a panoramic view of the surrounding treeless landscape. In the painting, one can see the top of the tabernacle at the Methodist campground and the church cross. It is a haunting, intriguing work of art.

Innisfail succumbed to a forest fire that burned the hotel to the ground in 1906, and the structure was never rebuilt. Only a cellar hole remains.

Across the Lagoon from the Oklahoma development is Hines Point, named for the investor Thomas Hines of New York. This development extended from Five Corners to the tip of the peninsula that protrudes into the Lagoon. Hines Point succeeded, in part, because Hines built a seven-hundred-foot bridge across the lagoon to the Vineyard Haven Road, which cost him $2,000. Today, the point is a vibrant community of private homes along a single roadway.

West Chop Cedars was a development initially planned in 1872 along the road to West Chop. There was a sense the project would not succeed unless it could connect to a public water supply and enjoy an improved roadway. Once the development was connected to Holmes Hole with a crushed-shell roadway—a highlight of the community—and town water, "West Chop soon became a summer retreat of houses, an inn, a community center called the Casino, tennis courts, and even a wharf with a private steamer running regularly to the mainland." West Chop Cedars boasted its own post office, which serviced the community, summers only, for nearly a century.[36]

Makoniky Heights, along Lambert's Cove Road, was proposed in 1891, built in 1893 and closed the same year. This short-lived project included a three-story hotel boasting twenty guest rooms, a wharf leading into Vineyard Sound and fifteen small cottages. The project began in the late spring of 1893, the year of the great financial panic, and the hotel opened that summer. Because the workers had not been paid, the doors were shuttered in August. (A later project to make bricks was planned on the site, including tracks to transport the product to ships on the shore. When it was determined the clay was inadequate to bond into bricks, the project was abandoned.)

The Bellevue Hotel was near the corner of Temahigan and New York Avenue on East Chop. It was later converted to the Treat Preparatory School for Boys. All that is visible today are three stone steps along Temahigan.

Bellevue Heights was a four-hundred-acre land development community with lots designated for house construction along New York Avenue under the proprietorship of Tarleton Cadwallader Luce. Although paper streets were laid out and plans developed, the organization filed for bankruptcy in February 1874, only three years after business began.

In 1974, the Strock family sought to develop a five-hundred-acre section on the shore of Sengekontacket with 824 house lots. The predecessor to the Martha's Vineyard Commission denied the plans. That site, Ocean Heights, was home to the Martha's Vineyard Country Club on Farm Pond. It was purchased, reconfigured and renamed Farm Neck Golf Course in 1979, with development for fifty homes, land donated to Felix Neck and conservation easements on the property.

The island of Chappaquiddick was not immune from development. As early as 1889, the so-called Enos Lots were established by Joseph Enos on fifty acres but never drew much attention. The Chappaquiddick Land Company and Chappaquiddick Camp were formed in 1890. Both developments were founded, faltered and folded without fanfare. Another projected development, Washqua Farm, consisted of two hundred acres on Pocha Pond.

An observation tower was erected on Samson's Hill southwest of the meeting house. Today, only a small marker denotes this highest point on Chappy.

Seaview City was a planned development between Caleb's Pond and Samson's Hill. It would have been conspicuous from Edgartown, and about 125 lots were sold.

Lots were laid out on the Wasque shoreline for a projected development in 1912. Chappaquiddick by the Sea began selling 775 house lots in 1913. Only a few were sold, and that was fortuitous, as much of the land has eroded into the sea over the last century.

Henry Hough pointed out that the balance between conservation and development was underway, and both concerns were worthy of consideration in how the future of the island was shaped. In 1935, Hough wrote, "Most lovers of Chappaquiddick rejoice that it is still elemental, without communities of cottages and hotels."

By Hough's calculations, there were about twenty-five houses in 1797, with two hundred inhabitants, of which seventy-five were Indians. In 1935, "there are fewer houses today, fewer inhabitants, and almost no Indians at all." Recently, former post office employee Angela Cywinski delivered mail in the winter to 65 mailboxes on Chappaquiddick; in the fall or shoulder season, that number rose to 125, and in the height of summer, with visitors, tourists and homeowners in residence, she would stop at 375 mailboxes. The population of Chappaquiddick has grown exponentially since the dawn of the twentieth century.[37]

APART FROM THE DOWN-ISLAND (Edgartown, Oak Bluffs and Vineyard Haven) land development projects that were enacted—and often failed—one man chose up-island (West Tisbury, Chilmark and Gay Head) as a summer refuge. "That first summer guest up-island was a most interesting person who had given up a prosperous hardware business in Cincinnati to marry Lucy Stone, one of the pioneers in the movement for women suffrage." Henry Blackwell was that person.[38]

Chilmark consisted of woodlots and farms, where locals raised corn, rye and oats. Henry and Lucy Blackwell bought farmland in Chilmark in the 1860s and became the first up-island summer visitors.

Henry Blackwell was a hardware magnate. Lucy Stone (1818–1893) made her name as a suffragette, an abolitionist and the first Massachusetts woman to earn a college degree. The couple purchased their house in 1864 and spent all of their summers in Chilmark.

Two of Blackwell's brothers also bought homes in Chilmark, and three sisters were summer guests. "At one point it almost looked as though the Blackwells would take over the town of Chilmark, but they didn't, for too many other off-islanders also discovered the beauty of up-island."

Henry Whiting was a scientist and cartographer who worked for the government, plotting maps of mid-nineteenth-century America. He created a detailed map of Martha's Vineyard, including water depths, island forestation and house lots. The 1850 Whiting Map is a masterpiece of description and clarification of the natural flora and human footprint on the Vineyard in the mid-nineteenth century.

Nathanial Shaler (1841–1906) was a Harvard professor—a geologist intrigued with paleontology. He was an ardent supporter of slavery and believed in the superiority of the white race. Curious about the geological anomalies of Martha's Vineyard, he settled on the island and studied the landscape, from rock formations to the lay of the land. He purchased property across from Fisher's Mill on North Road in what became West Tisbury. Whenever he returned to his house, he had to dismount from his horse and open and close a gate. This happened seven times en route to his house, hence the appellation "Seven Gates."

Shaler developed a summer retreat at Seven Gates, purchasing an adjacent old farmstead in 1888, and subsequently bought other homesteads on the one-thousand-acre site. Rather than divide the property into several house lots, he morphed his secluded property into an exclusive development among few landowners. As Henry Hough wrote in 1935, "The owners of summer homes on Seven Gates became members of a community which controlled and preserved the great estate." Today, Seven Gates is an organization with approximately thirty-five houses of five acres each, separate and removed from one another.[39]

Ichabod Luce lived in a house in Eastville near the proposed Bellevue Heights development. His house overlooked the pier that extended into Vineyard Haven Harbor on East Chop Drive, where the New York Yacht Club convened each year. Luce was active in local politics, concerned about the financial fallibility of the proposed Martha's Vineyard Railroad and advocated secession from Edgartown.

Due to the popularity of the Eastville pier and its ferry to New York, as well as the Yacht Club's annual visit, Kedron Avenue, the main street that ran out of Cottage City to Eastville was renamed New York Avenue. It retains that name to this day.

Development of the land of Martha's Vineyard was key in catering to the wants and needs of the tourist population. If tourists fell in love on their first or second Vineyard visit, it was propitious to sell them property; then they would want to build a house, especially as lots were numerous and inexpensive.

With its ten parks and one thousand house lots, Oak Bluffs is credited as the first planned community in the United States. While Erastus Carpenter is rightly praised for initiating this development, his Oak Bluffs Land & Wharf Company outlived its productivity. As Henry Hough commented, "Oak Bluffs as a resort community was on the highroad of favor; but Oak Bluffs as a land development had already lasted beyond its natural term." It folded in 1882.[40]

The land development plans did not always succeed; however, the schemes and proposals showed a determination by businessmen to take advantage of a second wave of tourists by promoting the options and opportunities of homeownership in a seaside community.

6

SECOND TOURIST WAVE (1880–1900)

Itseemstobewellunderstoodthatallwhocomehere[OakBluffs]eithercome
hungryorgethungryverysoonaftercoming,andsomebodymustdothefeeding.[41]
—Tours and Guide to Southern Massachusetts

The onslaught of tourists making their way to Martha's Vineyard in the mid-eighteenth century began with the Wesleyan Grove Camp Meeting Association. The Oak Bluffs Land & Wharf Company set the tone for land development projects with its planned community. What followed was a deluge of vacationers, tourists, adventurers and curiosity seekers who made the trek across Vineyard Sound to experience this unique summer resort that evolved in the last quarter of the nineteenth century.

Martha's Vineyard had arrived.

Reliable steamship service met the basic transportation needs of this influx of tourists, and with eighteen hotels in Cottage City, accommodations were generally sufficient for the growing tourist population. Restaurants sought to meet the needs of the hungry tourist, as the Tourist Guide of 1889 averred. And sufficient activities were offered across Martha's Vineyard, from the amusement park atmosphere in Cottage City to shoreline beaches, quaint villages like the county seat in Edgartown to the historic clay cliffs of Gay Head. There was a lot to see and do on Martha's Vineyard at the turn of the century, and many people wanted to be part of that experience.

Promoted and publicized as the Cottage City of America, the town had a year-round population of 570. When the Methodists and visiting tourists congregated for the summer, the population swelled to 20,000. (In 2020, 18,000 year-round residents live on Martha's Vineyard, with 125,000 additional summer people on any given day in July and August.) And during Camp Meeting week in August 1900, there would be as many as 40,000 people, all savoring the seaside charm of the island community. Historian Henry Beetle Hough observed that "Wesleyan Grove now draws its thousands from the whole populous east of the United States, and stragglers from afar. It is known all over the country—no, all over the world. It is the largest and most famous of all the camp meetings, and its fame is growing."[42]

By the middle of the nineteenth century, the Martha's Vineyard Camp Meeting Association attracted throngs of people. To bring these fervent Methodists to Wesleyan Grove required an efficient transportation system. As steam engines improved, railroad trains brought revivalists on the tracks to Woods Hole, where steamships transported the hoards to the bustling Methodist campground community each summer.

The Martha's Vineyard Railroad was key to the spread of tourism. Tourists rode between Oak Bluffs and Edgartown. Courtesy of the Connie Sanborn collection.

During one busy August day in 1860, Eagle's Wing and the Island Home brought 2,600 ardent Methodists and their acolytes to the Vineyard. Similarly, the Monohansett transported 1,400 passengers to the Vineyard in the morning and 1,800 back to the mainland on the evening of Sunday, August 28, 1863.

Pamphlets, booklets and newspaper accounts of the wonders of the Vineyard sang unfettered praise of the Vineyard's virtues. "The bathing facilities are excellent," crowed one booklet, reveling in the fine fishing and safe, friendly atmosphere. "Large steamers pass and repass several times a day, while the ocean is oftentimes literally covered with sailing craft of almost every description."[43]

Revivalism sponsored this great expansion of tourism. As more people came to the Methodist campground, more tourists, curiosity seekers and excursionists visited the Vineyard to savor the natural seashore and charming landscape promoted in tourist guides, ripe with enthusiastic declarations of Vineyard wonders.

The Vineyard Grove Company added another pier, Highland Wharf, in 1871, specifically for the Methodist Camp Meeting Association. Highland Wharf was adjacent to the Highland Hotel—site of the present East Chop Beach Club. This pier was used by the Camp Meeting Association and later by patrons of the Baptist tabernacle in the Highlands. "The purpose was symbolic, to allow those destined for the campground to disembark with dignity via a route especially designed to circumvent the more worldly parts of this growing resort community." The amusement park atmosphere was so near that it was feared it might entice wayward Methodists. For those patrons who sought to indulge in the vagaries of bathing beaches, ice cream parlors and candy shops, temptation was less than half a mile away.[44]

With sufficient ferry service across Vineyard Sound and three wharves along the East Chop shoreline to meet steamships, passengers who debarked in Cottage City needed transportation to various parts of town.

The Vineyard Grove Company developed a horsecar route from the Highland House Wharf along Commercial Street, also known as East Chop Drive, to the Camp Meeting Association. Now Methodist revivalists and their luggage traveled by horsecar directly into the Methodist campground on the shores of Sunset Lake. This avoided the attractions and distractions of nearby Cottage City. Today, tracks from this early trolley system are embedded in front of the Camp Meeting Administration building.

When President Grant visited Martha's Vineyard in August 1874, he traveled aboard a three-car private train to Woods Hole. From there, the president and his party crossed Vineyard Sound aboard the River Queen, landing at the Highland Wharf then boarded the horse-drawn trolley into the grounds of the Camp Meeting Association.

The tourist business extended beyond Woods Hole as word of the Vineyard spread up and down the coast. The welcoming tourist environment of Martha's Vineyard generated a reputation so great that steamship companies from other coastal states, Rhode Island, New York and Maine, scheduled stops at the Vineyard for day excursions or regular ports of call.

A popular excursion aboard steamboats from Cottage City was a daytrip down Vineyard Sound to Gay Head. One morbid highlight was viewing the wreck of the City of Columbus that ran aground on Devil's Bridge in 1884. When ashore, day-trippers would ride ox-carts, admire and even climb the multicolored clay cliffs and tour the brick lighthouse. This service brought tourist dollars to cash-strapped Gay Head, which was isolated from the rest of the island by inadequate roadways and a great distance. Steamships on an excursion to Gay Head entertained passengers with food and drink, geology lectures and often a brass band. The cost of such an all-day expedition in the 1880s was fifty cents.

WHEN SHUBAEL NORTON "CONCEIVED the idea of mapping out his land for purposes of sale, deeming this a suitable location for a summer resort," he exhibited the foresight that the land adjacent to the Camp Meeting Association would make a good summer development.

The Oak Bluffs Land & Wharf Company was to be commended for "the position which they took in the matter for furnishing amusements for the public in the way of illuminations, public games, and such events." And one of the primary events was making the beachfront shoreline the centerpiece of the development.[45]

Shubael Norton proceeded to construct bathhouses along the beach in front of Ocean Park for the cottage owners in the new development. Norton plumbed solar-heated saltwater showers that proved popular with tourists, as well as the Methodists of Wesleyan Grove during Camp Meeting week.

Bathhouses lined the beach in Oak Bluffs. (In 1933, the name Pay Beach was attributed to the site, as it cost a nickel a day to change from street clothes to bathing suit.) The bathhouses were blown down in the hurricane of 1944 and were never rebuilt.

Swimming proved a popular shoreline activity, also referred to as "dipping into the sea." Albion Hart of Oak Bluffs recalled, "All our bathing suits were

The North Bluff bandstand on the plank walkway offered a unique perspective on the steamship pier. Postcard courtesy of Arne Carr.

Pay Beach by Ocean Park in Oak Bluffs earned its moniker for the charge to use the bathhouse. Courtesy of the Connie Sanborn collection.

wool. And we were not allowed to walk through the streets in our bathing suits." After hanging his suit in the bathhouse overnight, he would find it cold, wet and clammy the next day. Hart recalled that when his mother was at the beach, "you'd have thought she was going to a fancy-dress ball." Besides a taffeta hat, she wore black stockings, bloomers, sandals and a top with long sleeves and ruffles that blossomed in the water. He added, "We swam every day. There were two showers, one fresh water and the other salt, which was supposed to be healthy for you."

A 3,500-foot-long plank walkway stretched from Highland Wharf to the shore of the Inkwell. "Bluffing" was the appellation assigned to the romantic stroll a couple might enjoy along that lengthy plank boardwalk— to saunter along, hand in hand, listening to band music wafting out along the shore.

Kids would dive for coins off the steamship dock. (As late as the 1970s, local kids would dive for coins. Kenny Ivory recalled that as a youngster he would kneel at low tide on the ocean floor, waving his arms, to seek a tossed coin.) Many teenagers enjoyed hanging out at Lover's Rock in the water by the beach. And the pavilion along the boardwalk served food and drink.

Not everyone was impressed by the attire seen on the beaches of Cottage City. "A bathing house is a great disenchanter, and in a moment or two, can scatter most thoroughly the fondest dream of beauty and remove the mask from face and form, perhaps, startling and not always pleasing disclosures," complained the Island Review.[46]

Adults did not swim in the late 1800s, only children, and it was considered bathing not swimming. "The editor has his own opinion of why no gentlelady would wear a styling bathing suit. It would attract attention, something no lady of the 1870s would ever want at the beach." The reviewer added, "Why the popular bathing suit should be as unnecessarily ugly as it is, we leave to those who use them."[47]

CROQUET WAS ONE OF the more popular nonreligious campground activities in the 1870s. The game flourished to the point of dominating activity unrelated to the Methodist prayer meetings. Young people would stake their wickets early in the day and play whenever the opportunity arose. Older, more sedate players appreciated the slower pace of croquet, gently knocking their wooden ball through the wicket and relishing the game's peaceful tranquility. On occasion, rivalries between revivalists arose over who set the game up first, which caused consternation among the brethren.

Croquet reigned supreme in the campground. Ladies were said to surreptitiously move the ball, hidden beneath long skirts. Courtesy of the Martha's Vineyard Museum.

Waban Park was another center for croquet. The Martha's Vineyard Croquet Club, founded in 1890, ensured the game enjoyed a prominent place in the tourist community. Croquet cost nothing to organize or play but attracted attention as participants were inspired by the social pleasure of the game and appreciated the calming shore-front atmosphere.

Another activity that occurred with neither promotion nor expense was the advent of a different sort of tourist: bicycle riders, known as wheelmen, visited Martha's Vineyard in the latter part of the nineteenth century.

In 1871, the high wheel bike was popular among young men but could easily tip if the rider hit a stone in the road. Ladies with long skirts found it a challenge to ride. In 1884, the chain and sprocket came into use and was popular with children and the elderly because the chain propelled the back wheel rather than the high front wheel.

The Capital Bicycle Club from Washington, D.C., rode in Cottage City in 1885. Two years later, the Massachusetts division of the League of American Wheelmen came to Cottage City for its "summer rendezvous." This established a pattern of unsolicited tourist activity for more than a decade, which added to the excitement of the community. In 1895, more than two hundred wheelmen pedaled through town. And in their finale, the wheelmen rode illuminated bicycles in a parade through Cottage City.

Wheelmen from clubs along the East Coast were attracted to the high-quality concrete roadways in Cottage City, which included thirty miles of pavement. "Concreted with a tar preparation" meant cyclists could ride in clusters over long stretches of level roadways. And they could pedal very fast. It proved an exciting exercise.

For some wheelmen, their excitement got out of hand, and one year, the wheelmen were banished to Vineyard Haven due to their rowdiness. Apparently, they were offered a reprieve and returned to Cottage City, where the roadways were better. They promised to behave.

In the late 1880s, wheelmen became a Vineyard fixture, and the prowess of riding bicycles on island pavement promoted the Vineyard in a way no one anticipated. The annual Tivoli Day races of cyclists drew enthusiastic wheelmen, who rhapsodized about the idyllic biking in Cottage City.

In the 1890s, when the Martha's Vineyard Railroad track ran parallel to the road, bikers proved faster than the Active, the engine pulling the little train across the Vineyard.

Another spectator sport that intrigued both locals and tourists was whaleboat races. As the whaling industry declined following the Civil War, the great whaleships were abandoned, and the whaleboats—the thirty-foot rowing craft used to capture whales—were scattered about the shoreline. These boats became the genesis of whaleboat racing.

The first race was rowed in 1875 among eight boats from New Bedford and the Vineyard and was crewed by retired whalemen. As in the actual whaling experience, each whaleboat held six men: three oars on one side, two oars on the other and the captain steered with a long oar in the stern. A New Bedford whaleboat won that race. More races followed that summer, and the competition garnered national interest. Over the years, it became an annual tradition in Cottage City, coinciding with Illumination Night. A reported seven thousand people lined the shores to watch a whaleboat race in 1876, again won by New Bedford.

Vineyard boatbuilder Uriah Morse, whose family operated the Chappy ferry in the mid-1800s, designed a custom whaleboat with unsupported oak thwarts (seats). "When the men pulled, their springy seats pulled the sides of the boat in, making it a little narrower and so a little faster." Oak Bluffs won that race. (That boat is housed in the Martha's Vineyard Museum in Vineyard Haven.)[48]

Whaleboat races continued into the 1890s, creating an exciting opportunity for islanders and tourists to share in the excitement of the contest.

Before hayrides, straw rides proved a popular tourist treat. "The straw rides of yore were loud, fast, raucous, late-night, teenage events, prone to romance, drama, and a whole lot of noise." Often, hotels organized the straw rides so the tourist could appreciate the experience. There were an "equal number of gentlemen and ladies who have arranged in advance who goes with who, and there is always a married lady along as chaperon." A moonlit night worked best, and the wagon was crowded with a group of two dozen or so people, equipped with a few cymbals and guitars and peanuts or candy to tide them over.[49] The straw wagon was driven rapidly through the streets, accompanied by jingling bells and raucous singing by the young people engaged in an evening of excitement. Straw rides were a pleasurable activity for the young who participated, lying on their backs, searching the heavens and spending time with their peers on a romantic adventure.

Straw rides attained the height of popularity in the 1890s, with rides through Edgartown down to South Beach. Again, this activity could be appreciated by both locals and visitors and proved an exciting way to enjoy the out-of-doors on a moonlit night on Martha's Vineyard.

Another activity that involved horses was a racetrack. On the Fourth of July in 1873, a half-mile track for trotting horses opened at Girdlestone Park in the middle of Martha's Vineyard. (Ruins of the stands lie in the woods to the right of Deer Run North.) This horseracing operation attracted tourists from off-island, as well as a hearty number of island stalwarts. Steamships traveled to the head of the lagoon and dropped off passengers, so the bettors walked less than half a mile to the track. For nearly forty years, Girdlestone was a hidden hive of activity nestled in the heart of Martha's Vineyard.

Not all of the aspects of the amusement park atmosphere fostered in Cottage City were without advertising or expense. Several innovative rides and carnival-type activities were introduced to the Cottage City crowds of tourists in the 1880s.

The Flying Horses carousel was designed and built for Coney Island in 1878. It was moved to the Vineyard in 1884, situated high on the bluff beyond the steamship slip near the present Lookout Restaurant. Cost of this merry-go-round ride was five cents, and the experience was advertised as "Fun for the Old Folks as well as for the Children." After a few years, it was deemed the structure was too close to the ocean, and in 1889, the Flying Horses was relocated to its present location in Farland Square. Today, the Flying Horses continues to amuse young children and amaze adults, who

Girdlestone Racetrack thrived into the early 1900s. Today, this open field is a reminder of a bygone era. Courtesy of Joyce Dresser.

linger to listen to the calliope music and hope their youngster manages to catch the brass ring to earn another circular adventure on this, the oldest continuously operating (in the summer) carousel in the United States.

Roller-skating was great fun in the latter part of the nineteenth century. Samuel Winslow built the first roller-skating rink in the central Massachusetts city of Worcester in 1876. He then constructed a massive roller rink on the island adjacent to the Sea View House. The Vineyard Skating Rink opened in 1879 in the heart of the community—at the current site of Santander Bank. The roller rink, or casino, boasted cupolas and towers, an arched roof and hanging lanterns illuminating the rink. It was a fixture in Cottage City for more than a decade. An audience of up to one thousand people could watch the activity. Bands played at the casino. Children and adults rolled merrily along. It was a big deal.

Winslow raised roller-skating to a new height. He expanded the sport when he developed a unique design for his skate, known as the Vineyard Special. It was better designed and quickly attained popularity along the East Coast; by its name alone, the Vineyard Special drew attention to Martha's Vineyard. "In the rink the summer dwellers of Cottage City discovered anew the swift joy of motion…the next thing to flying." And roller-skating came to be considered "a convenient adjunct of the simpler and more national recreation of bluffing," that leisurely stroll along the shoreline boardwalk. On the Vineyard, activities included social skating, tricks and roller polo. In the years 1883 and 1884, the rink flourished with a variety of activity. Tourists could skate at one of the three daily sessions for 25 cents, which included renting the skates. Fancy skating shows were promoted.[50]

Two Cottage City teams competed in a roller-skating polo tournament. One program featured "Miss Carrie A. Gilmore, of Worcester, the acknowledged champion lady skater in the country. This is Miss Gilmore's first appearance before a Cottage City audience." Another show promoted Professor Daniel Canary on a "monocycle," where he "will perform the wonderful feat of riding one wheel (devoid of all attachments) backwards, an act never before attempted at the Rink." According to one report from the era, the Vineyard roller-skating rink "was the first real roller skating rink in the country and accounts for the name Vineyard being applied to the skates."[51]

In 1892, the Sea View House burned, taking down the Vineyard Skating Rink as well, and that was the end of roller-skating in Oak Bluffs.

The skating rink was an imposing structure. The Vineyard special skate popularized the island in the late 1800s. Courtesy of the Martha's Vineyard Museum.

A Toboggan Slide was erected near the casino in 1887—the first of its kind in New England. It featured a tall, gently sloping 850-foot-long ride. The structure created an immediate sensation by its expansive physical appearance and the sensation of riding on a roller coaster. However, it did not prove popular, and in a few short seasons, the toboggan slide lost its appeal and was demolished.

In the 1880s, a seventy-five-foot-high observation tower was erected along Ocean Park and became a stop on the railroad. This was a highlight for visitors, as it offered a view of the village of Cottage City, as well as the waters of Vineyard Sound and across to Cape Cod. By 1895, it had lost its appeal and it, too, was torn down.

Adjacent to the observation tower on Ocean Park, the beachfront community blossomed over the years but not without controversy. Bathhouses were extended in height above the bluff, which led to a lawsuit that was settled by Judge Oliver Wendell Holmes in 1902. His ruling ensured that the ocean view must be protected and that the sight was "dedicated" to the

This gradual toboggan slide was a short-lived amusement. Tourists soon tired of it and moved on. Courtesy of the Martha's Vineyard Museum.

A plank walkway stretched more than half a mile along the shoreline, inviting excursionists to stroll along its wide expanse. This was termed "bluffing" back in the day. Courtesy of the Martha's Vineyard Museum.

cottagers. Hence no bathhouses, pavilions or towers could rise above the bluff to obstruct the view across Ocean Park.

When a tourist or local needed a break from the entertainment and excitement all around, savoring ice cream on Circuit Avenue was a delightful treat. For a young child, sitting on a stool at Rauche's soda fountain in the Metropolitan Hotel had to rank as one of the true pleasures of a summer visit at the turn of the century.

Ruth Eldridge recalled the anticipation of "our evening spree we had been looking to since winter." After riding the trolley from Vineyard Haven, "the remaining thirty [cents of fifty] had to cover rides on the Flying Horses [with luck, you'd catch the brass ring for an extra ride or two], a popcorn bar at Darling's, and a fifteen-cent dish of ice cream at Rausch's." Ice cream was tops. "The last was a dream of elegance come true, for when we were seated around the marble-topped table, in would come a handsome young man in a white coat to take our order. He would bring tall glasses of ice water for each of us and colorful paper napkins." Her memories continued, "When the tray of ice cream arrived, there would be a plate of sultana fruit cookies, which the waiter with a dignified flourish would place in the center of the table." Ruth recalled, "We were careful to eat our ice cream with our little finger curled so that anyone who looked at us might be impressed."[52]

Ruth Eldridge commented on the role Cottage City played "as a spectacularly popular summer resort, brought into being and to a large extent sustained by the great religious revival meetings that encamped there in the latter part of the 1800s. Oak Bluffs had big hotels, restaurants, fine shops, and even a railway train to shuttle people to and from the broad sandy beaches on the south shore."[53]

WHILE THE MAJORITY OF tourists were middle-class New Englanders, a number of wealthy patrons sought a place to embark on their vacation and socialize with their fellow titans of industry. A number of prominent Boston tycoons organized the Train Club and approached the Old Colony Railroad with a request: they would guarantee a certain income for the railroad if they could ride a private fast train from Boston to Woods Hole. The so-called dude train ran from 1884 through the summer of 1916, "whisking wealthy Bostonians at unprecedented speeds and with unsurpassed luxury from their city offices to their summer retreats on Cape Cod and the Islands." (In the late nineteenth century, the term dude referred to a fashionable gentleman.) President Cleveland rode the dude train. This "seasonal, private, posh weekday" train took elite vacationers to their summer homes in time for cocktails and dinner.

The dude train was officially listed as a private train; it consisted of a baggage/smoking car and two drawing room cars. It left Boston promptly at 3:10 p.m. and arrived at 4:50 p.m. in Woods Hole to return the next morning. Patrons paid $100 a season ($2,500 today) plus train fare for the opportunity to embark on this venture. The train averaged more than forty miles per hour and made limited stops, only where a tycoon had his summer home.

The demise of the dude train came about with the arrival of the automobile and the onset of World War I. Regular train service from Boston continued to Woods Hole until 1964. And when that service ended, the southern spur was converted into a bicycle path—the Shining Sea Bikeway.

Passengers of the dude train were not the only wealthy patrons heading to the Vineyard. A group of seven dissatisfied millionaire fishermen from Sakonnet Point, Rhode Island, broke from their local fishing group to found a fishing club on Cuttyhunk, one of the Elizabeth Islands west of Martha's Vineyard. For $4,000, they bought the west end of the island and built the Cuttyhunk Fishing Club in 1865.

The men paid $1.50 per day for a bedroom, with an adjacent bath appointed with a small round metal tub. When a millionaire sat on the edge of the tub, his "man" poured water over him for a personal shower. There was a dining salon, a porch and terraces but no women. The club paid to have a well dug with a pump house, storage tank and icehouse. Sport fishing was off twenty-six stands that were set in the water each summer.

Cuttyhunk guests included President Grover Cleveland and Hugh Auchincloss, stepfather of Jackie Onassis. Jay Gould fished there. A diamond-studded fishhook was awarded to the man who caught the largest fish each year. A forty-seven-pound striped bass won in 1870 and a sixty-four-pound bass in 1884.

The heyday of the club was from 1865 to 1912. The Cuttyhunk Fishing Club proved an economic boon to the island of Cuttyhunk. Today, guests may stay in a room at the Cuttyhunk Fishing Club Family Bed-and-Breakfast to relive the tradition of bygone years.

On occasion, fishermen ventured from one idyllic fishing site to another. The following account, written by tourist Francis Endicott, was published in Scribner's Magazine in 1881: "A bright August morning found the writer, in company with a member of the Cuttyhunk Club, steaming down the bay from New Bedford, bound for a trip to the Elizabeth Islands and Martha's Vineyard, and for a bout with the large bass which frequent the rocky shores of those favored regions." The first excitement was passing a cluster of sword fishing boats in Cuttyhunk harbor. After a night at the Cuttyhunk Fishing Club, frequented by business tycoons, the party headed to Martha's Vineyard.

Due to strong winds, the intrepid travelers opted to take the steamship from Woods Hole, and then "we steam away for the headlands of Martha's Vineyard, visible in the distance, and in due time haul up at the wharf of that marvelous city of cottages, and take the stage to commence a tedious journey the full length of the island, some twenty-two miles." After crossing streams filled with brook trout, the anglers learned the stage coach did not travel to Gay Head, so they "boarded a buggy, with a bright school-boy of some thirteen summers as a driver, whom we ply with questions as to the names of localities passed on the route."

Following a delightful sightseeing experience in Gay Head, appreciating the lighthouse, the varigated clay cliffs and the glacial erratic along the shore, the anglers set out to fish for bass using lobster meat as bait and were rewarded with numerous fish. Wanting to stay another day, they realized their catch would not keep, so the travelers headed home. Endicott stated, "Our trip is over, and we pack our things to return home. Stored in a box, carefully packed with broken ice, are five bass,—we take no account of two bluefish of eight and ten pounds."[54]

According to Vineyard angler/historian Kib Bramhall, "Several exclusive striped bass clubs were started along the New England coast, organized by some of the most prominent citizens of the time. One of the most famous was the Squibnocket Club, formed in 1869 on the cliffs of Squibnocket Point in Chilmark." Many of the members were among the New York business elite and included Presidents Grover Cleveland and Chester Arthur and naturalist Dr. Louis Agassiz. Bramhall notes, "Affairs of state and industry were settled in the clubhouse—libation in hand—after the day's catch had been weighed, and instructions were dispatched to Washington and Wall Street by the club's carrier pigeons." The Squibnocket Club brought a manservant, Squibnocket Willie, to meet the anglers' every need, from baiting a hook with lobster meat to fetching a refreshing mint julep.[55]

Another group of industrialists from Rhode Island formed the Providence Club, also on Squibnocket shores, adjacent to the present bridge and parking lot. These two clubs proved popular into the 1880s, when bass fishing was superb. The best year was 1875, when a dozen forty-pound bass were caught. And early autumn, especially September, was considered the most successful time for bass fishing.

In 1926, the Hornblower family purchased the shoreline, and a quarter century later, a revived fishing club was formed, the Squibnocket Bass and Surf Club. Off-island fishermen continue to savor the social camaraderie of bass fishing along the scenic shoreline of Martha's Vineyard, as they have for over a century and half.

As Martha's Vineyard eased into the last decade of the nineteenth century, the economics of a resort community came into play, especially in Cottage City. Along with extensive land development projects selling and settling large swaths of Vineyard acreage, the resort community focused on a different direction, enticing tourists to stay in hotels and boardinghouses in Cottage City and across the Vineyard. To supplement the hotel trade, entrepreneurs devised entertainment opportunities to entice visitors in amusements of all kinds. Tourists sampled and savored various entertainments in the down-island communities.

One form of amusement and locomotion was the Martha's Vineyard Railroad, which continued to chug back and forth between Cottage City and Edgartown between 1874 and 1895.

The one thousand house lots of the Oak Bluffs Land & Wharf Company had been sold. Many lots already boasted new houses, designed in the Queen

Anne style. Rooms at the Sea View House in Cottage City were often full. Even the Mattakeeset Hotel in Katama enjoyed the fruits of success brought by railroad passengers. Yet it was time, and the Oak Bluffs Land & Wharf Company closed in 1882.

In the 1890s, many of the "the outstanding figures in the summer resort development of Martha's Vineyard passed from the scene, and their era ended with a sharpness of definition which is often lacking in human affairs."[56]

The following men contributed a great deal to the resort community and passed away in the last decade of the nineteenth century:

Hebron Vincent (1890) chronicled the history of the Camp Meeting Association.

Ichabod Luce (1894) fought against the railroad and for secession of Cottage City from Edgartown.

Dr. Harrison Tucker (1894) earned a reputation as a prominent person in the community.

Samuel Osborn (1895) was an influential whaleship owner and supporter of the railroad. His private home became the Charlotte Inn in Edgartown.

William Bradley (1895) was a founder of the Oak Bluffs Land & Wharf Company.

Shubael Norton (1901) invested in the Oak Bluffs Land & Wharf Company. His monument in Oak Grove cemetery towers over nearby graves.

Erastus Carpenter (1902) founded the Oak Bluffs Land & Wharf Company, establishing Cottage City.

Concurrent with the deaths of prominent promoters, several arson fires occurred, primarily in hotels, which fractured the fragile financial framework of the tourist community already weakened by the Panic of 1893. Businesses and land development projects folded through bankruptcy or failed to meet the needs of tourists and investors.

Late in the evening of September 4, 1892, a raging fire was discovered in the massive Sea View House in the heart of Cottage City. While there were no injuries, damage to the hotel was extensive. The adjacent casino was engulfed in flames as the Vineyard Skating Rink burned. The Steamship wharf burned, and the Martha's Vineyard Railroad's roundhouse was destroyed. Henceforth, the railroad engine could not turn around, so it ran forward to Cottage City, then backed toward Edgartown.

Other hotels suffered mysterious torchings in subsequent years. The Highland House burned in October 1893. The Cottage City School and five cottages burned in the campground in 1894. The Wesley Hotel (today known as Summercamp) was set afire on November 13, 1894, but the owner, Augustus Wesley, was apprehended after he was seen setting the blaze. He served three years in jail for attempted arson. The Prospect House Hotel by the lagoon burned in 1898.

It is worth an aside to credit Holder Brownell, manager of the Sea View House for seventeen years, for his role in promoting the facility and hosting numerous prominent people: President Grant, Vice President (under Grant) and Senator Henry Wilson, Vice President (under Hayes) William Wheeler, Justice Oliver Wendell Holmes, publisher of the New York Herald James Gordon Bennett, Massachusetts governors Alexander Hamilton Rice and Thomas Talbot, General Joseph Hooker and General Benjamin Franklin Butler.

Tourists, vacationers, summer people and prominent personalities continued to visit Martha's Vineyard. "Most of the multitudes which thronged the streets at the season-end celebrations were transients, excursionists coming for the day or for a weekend; yachtsmen; and guests of the regular summer residents."[57]

The little village of Cottage City embraced the end of the nineteenth century, acknowledging significant changes in the community but still reveling in its role as the hub of tourism.

7

Turn-of-the-Century Tourism (1900)

[A tourist guide's purpose was] first, to aid the tourist and stranger and direct him quickly to the special points of interest in the famous summer places mentioned; to entertain him and help enliven his way on his journeyings.[58]
—Illustrated Travel Guide

I n 1937, the Vineyard Gazette reprised an account of a week-long summer activity held in Edgartown in August 1893. The Gazette interviewed some of the original participants to get their perspectives on that long-lost summer.[59]

The annual summer social witnessed "one round of events after another at Edgartown, afloat and ashore. There were races and field sports and socials of one kind or another." A tub race off the bathing beach drew a crowd of some four hundred people. First prize was a three-dollar silk umbrella.

The baseball game played near the jail drew another crowd. The Harbor Views defeated the town team. Catcher Philip Pent of the hotel observed, "The town team was pretty sore at me because I helped with the game for the summer people." The hotel guests gave Pent ten dollars for his services. Henry Jernigan played shortstop without a glove. Forty years later, he recalled few memories of that game from all those years ago.

The rowboat race "was one of the most enjoyable of the series of entertainments...with enthusiastic spectators" all about. Both single and double rowboats participated. The Harbor View hop proved popular. And there was a whist party that evening.

Tourists and locals competed in a week-long series of games and contests in Edgartown in 1893. Photograph by Richard Shute, courtesy of the Vineyard Gazette.

"The surf at South Beach attracted many during the heavy southerly gale of Tuesday, and trains went down loaded with passengers. The surf was by far the grandest of the season." Who knew participants could simply hop on the Martha's Vineyard Railroad and ride to South Beach to view the surf? Those were the days.

The weeklong program continued with road races Wednesday afternoon. "The street presented a very animated appearance, and Shute, photographer, was able to secure several negatives from which he has finished some very fine pictures which are on exhibition and for sale at his store."

Activities were varied and imaginative. A one-hundred-yard three-legged race proved exciting. The potato race was described as an event with "30 potatoes five feet apart, entailing a run of about 4,600 feet." A high jump was held, as well as a greased pig race in the courthouse lot.

And the Gazette duly reported that "Chester E. Pease had little memory of this event, but he did say that he was pretty lean and limber as a young man. Lyman Norton is judged to have been the best high jumper around at the period."

It may be hard to imagine staid Edgartownians prancing and dancing through these varied competitions. Probably many visitors or tourists looked on or participated. "Altogether the week has been big with sport and the several contests have been much enjoyed by hundreds," declared the author of the original 1893 Gazette article.

TOURISM THRIVED AT THE turn of the century, after decades of Vineyard visits by Methodist Camp Meeting adherents, Azorian immigrants and land speculators. The tourist economy followed the whaling economy, and Martha's Vineyard bustled and thrived with activity on several fronts. A few clips from the archives of the Vineyard Gazette in the late 1890s share the flavor of the era:

August 5, 1897:
"All the hotels and cottages at West Chop are occupied and everything indicates that '97 will prove a most prosperous and happy season with the dwellers on the bluff."

August 19, 1897:
"Go to Lake Tashmoo and take a row on the prettiest sheet of water you ever saw. There are boats to let at the pumping station."

"The town has more strangers in it than for years past, and we heard some one who ought to know say that Vineyard Haven is going to boom next season."

September 23, 1897:
"In the horse trotting contest at Whiting's track West Tisbury several heats in the various classes were trotted on Wednesday and the races were finished today. Messrs. Carl Lair, Leroy Norton, Benton Blankenship, Frank P. Norton, Orlin Davis, Bartlett Mayhew, each have fast horses entered."

"Quite a number of summer visitors still linger with us. They are loath to leave their homes beside the sea. We all-the-year-around residents feel and believe that this month and October are the fairest and the brightest of the year."

October 7, 1897:
"Moonlight bicycle riding is enjoyed by many of our young people."

February 2, 1898:
"The young people have had a fine time skating on Tashmoo. The ice boats have been out in force."

June 9, 1898:
"Innisfail has 30 guests at the present time. This is one of the most attractive spots on the Island, and we do not wonder that it is being liberally patronized."

September 29, 1898:
"We are glad to hear that many of our summer people will make their home here this winter."

In the 1937 Gazette, there was a piece on the peculiarities of travel, stating, "One summer visitor to Martha's Vineyard for almost a generation expressed his dissatisfaction with present means of transportation to the Vineyard with considerable force, the other day." The article noted that the visitor drove up from the South with no problem, but "in New York, lacking the New Bedford boat on which he had travelled in other years, he asked for accommodations on the Fall River Line. Sold out three weeks in advance. A compartment, then, on the Cape Codder, so that the family dog could make the trip with his master and mistress. Sold out two weeks in advance."

His traveling travails continued: "The trip was made by train, sans compartment, and an untoward feature of the journey was the necessity for going to dinner at 10:30 in the morning in order to insure getting a seat, and of then being served pancakes as the single choice of a meal available."

Tourists sometimes had to contend with the challenges of inadequate access to the Vineyard. Summer people, like the visitor who complained, found problems wherever they went. That was the world in 1937, and it's not so different today.

THE POPULARITY OF MARTHA'S Vineyard was unquestioned at the turn of the century, even with limited access. Had the retired whaling captains and land promoters not merged their capital and talent to develop the summer resort community, what would have become of Martha's Vineyard? Describing the dawn of the twentieth century, historian/author Henry Beetle Hough wrote with confidence that "Martha's Vineyard became a flourishing watering place, its revenues swollen by an undreamed of accession of summer visitors. Boardinghouses were patronized as never before, boats rented readily, houses were built, and tradesmen everywhere found new custom."[60]

Yet even as the ferries were crowded, the hotels booked and the amusement sites busy, a new culture was evolving among the visitors and summer people. As Hough put it, "there was a new regime in which summer residents formed clubs and associations to lay out golf courses and provide for their own entertainment."

Summer people tended to socialize among themselves rather than intermingle or integrate with the year-round population. "It is an inseparable part of the new outlook that social control shall vest in the members of the special summer order; the line is drawn against the world in general."[61]

By 1900, summer visitors, tourists and residents began to live separate, if parallel, lives.

8

Early Twentieth Century (1900–30)

The tradition was established early that Cottage City
should be the place of merrymaking.[62]

E very entertainment in Cottage City revolved around movement or
motion of some sort, from bicycle riding and the Flying Horses to
racing Thoroughbreds and the comely game of Roque. During this heyday
of tourism, a concerted effort was made to amuse the hordes of tourists who
had heard about the Vineyard, taken the time and paid the cost to cross
the sound and now wanted to experience the Vineyard firsthand. What did
these tourists want to see and do in the first years of the twentieth century?

In 1935, the Vineyard Gazette wrote rhapsodically about the memorable
days in 1905, when the little village of Cottage City was fully immersed
in amusement activities. "How the flying horses, flying automobiles, flying
tally-ho coaches and flying feet on the floor of the dancing pavilion make
Old Father Time fly!…Take your stand, if you please, on any part of Circuit
avenue as an observation point, and watch the ebb and flow of rest-seeking
humanity." A lot was going on in that exciting era, and vestiges of it are
extant today, though many of the more popular pastimes have faded into the
pages of history. Between 1880 and 1915, Cottage City reached the peak of
activities focused on amusing the endless stream of tourists who descended
on the tiny island town.

The amusement park atmosphere blossomed in Cottage City, with plenty
of entertainment for visitors. In other parts of the island, there was more

Circuit Avenue encircled the Oak Bluffs Land & Wharf Company development. It became the center of the summer resort community. Courtesy of the Connie Sanborn collection.

to do for the more well-to-do patron, although such activities were less boisterous than those in Cottage City.

Trolley routes expanded across Cottage City and connected with Vineyard Haven. The rolling, rollicking streetcars brought noise, color and pleasure to summer life, as well as the capability for tourists and locals to ride expeditiously and inexpensively from one part of town to another, exposing them to a broader swath of the quaint charms of the community.

In 1935, with all the modern means of transport (trains, planes and automobiles), Henry Beetle Hough observed, "There has never been a motion so peculiarly thrilling as the rocking of a small streetcar in its swift course over a clear stretch of track, say the down grade between Cottage City and Eastville. Or is it memory that makes it so?" The bygone days are glorified by our historical perspective of the halcyon days of yore.[63]

The island community was changing, evolving and facing challenges. A new population of tourists sought more varied activities for their entertainment and amusement. As the automobile made its appearance at the start of the new century, life on Martha's Vineyard began to change and adapt to the new wave of tourists and visitors.

This early-twentieth-century postcard depicts the Oak Bluffs pier jammed with horseless carriages. Courtesy of Abby Armstrong/Tuckernuck Antiques.

The curious tourist who drove over the unpaved state road twenty miles out to Gay Head was rewarded by the opportunity to meet members of the Wampanoag tribe. A token souvenir, like a clay pot or cup or vase, also made the trip memorable.

Some sought nourishment. Over the years, a number of enterprising tribal members opened restaurants and small hotels in Gay Head. In the early twentieth century, Herbert Vanderhoop ran the Not-a-Way and Vanderhoop restaurants decades before electricity reached Gay Head.

In the 1920s, the Nestle Nook homestead on Lobsterville Road accommodated tourists who sought a few relaxing days on the Gay Head peninsula. In 1987, the Duck Inn in the old Belain homestead opened to the tourist trade.

Back in Cottage City, renamed Oak Bluffs in 1907, the Tivoli Dance Hall flourished in the first quarter of the twentieth century. Built in 1907 across from the steamship pier in Oak Bluffs, at the site of the present Police Department, the Tivoli became a mecca for music and dancing, ice cream sundaes and souvenirs. And it housed a shooting gallery and a dancing bear. The Tivoli exemplified the amusement park atmosphere of Cottage City. "Easily identified by two towers, one at either end, the Tivoli was a large wooden structure, painted yellow. The second floor ballroom opened onto a wide veranda, which allowed dance music to flow outside."[64]

The Tivoli, Oak Bluffs, Mass.

This Tivoli postcard exhibits the popularity of the twentieth-century dance hall. Courtesy of the Martha's Vineyard Museum.

Big bands played the Tivoli with featured soloists. Jazz musicians ruled the stage, with swing as the most popular. Waltz music was in vogue. Composer Will Hardy led the house band, the Novelty Orchestra from Worcester. Hardy predominated at the Tivoli from 1915 to 1931. His "Tivoli Girl" was a staple of the era, as was Etta Godrey's "Oak Bluffs Galop."

"The bottom floor housed shops and an ice cream parlor. My godmother worked in the ice cream parlor and I always enjoyed visiting her there." So begins a blog by Joan Boyken, a summer visitor of Oak Bluffs in her childhood.

Joan recalled a special visit to the Tivoli. "I was 3 years old and had newly mastered winking and was anxious to put it to use. Sitting at a table behind my mother and facing me was a sailor. Being that I was wearing a sailor dress I figured we had something in common and so I began winking at him." This was Oak Bluffs in the 1940s.

Joan's mother turned as the young sailor approached their table. "He smiled and said he was alone on the Vineyard for the day and wanted to tell my mother how charming he thought I was." Joan admits to a slight embarrassment. "Not only did my mother invite him to join us at the table but she invited him home for dinner. I was amazed at how powerful this winking thing was."[65]

Dreamland competed with the Tivoli for the tourist crowd. It is reincarnated in its original formula to entertain tourists. Courtesy of Joyce Dresser.

The Cape Cod Times reported on the resurrection of another structure from the era of the Tivoli right across the street: "Around the time the Dreamland Ballroom was opened, the town became a vacation destination for secular revelers, too." Summer partygoers went wherever their hearts chose. "'There was this whole different reason for coming here then, and it was purely for pleasure,' Dana Street, library assistant at the Martha's Vineyard Museum, said.

"'The Dreamland Ballroom and other pleasure palaces, such as the well-known Tivoli Dance Hall, drew thousands of vacationers enjoying the freer, post-Victorian era,' she said. 'But the Dreamland was overshadowed by its neighbor, the Tivoli, and became the Dreamland Dancing and Moving Pictures hall by 1910.'" From a moving pictures gallery to a car garage and later a roller-skating rink and arcade, the Dreamland returned to its original position as a recreational restaurant in 2013.[66]

The beaches of Cottage City continued to be a source of pleasure for vacationers, tourists and the local summer population.

In 1925, the town of Oak Bluffs assumed ownership of the old Oak Bluffs Land & Wharf beach by eminent domain. The town managed the 638 bathhouses that were still in use at Pay Beach. By the next year, the beach had fallen into disrepair along Ocean Park from the Steamship pier to Town Beach/Inkwell. The town set about repairing the shoreline with a retaining wall and beautifying the park landscape to the best of its ability. Appearances matter, and townspeople took pride in their shoreline atmosphere.

An energetic group of property owners organized the Highlands Property Trust and, in 1933, bought the beach originally owned by Vineyard Grove; they then sold it to the town. The Highlands Property Trust assumed ownership of the Highland Bathing Beach by the wharf and built the structure known today as the East Chop Beach Club.

THE DIARY OF LOUISE Edgar explores a teenager's summer adventures in the early years of the twentieth century.

The Edgars came from New Jersey to the Vineyard in the summer and stayed at the Valentine Pease house in Edgartown. Louise Edgar was fourteen when she kept a diary in 1906.

Swimming was her favorite activity. Louise and her sister swam at Chadwick's Beach on Chappaquiddick, where the Beach Rules required that "bare legged women will not be tolerated. Must wear stockings, not socks. Bathing suit skirts must come to knees."

Louise became proficient in both rowing and sailing in Edgartown harbor. She helped out by mowing the lawn. In her diary, she wrote about being punished by not being allowed to read and once went into the woods with a girlfriend to read and eat candy.

Through the mail, Louise ordered a pair of roller skates and a new bathing suit over the course of her summer. For ten cents, she skated at the casino in Oak Bluffs, where a brass band played. She recalled "Popcorn" Harry sold Darling's Popcorn in Edgartown and previously had sold it on the railroad.

Louise kept a pet rabbit and made a cage for him. One day, the family took an all-day trip to Gay Head. In Cottage City, they attended a baseball game between Edgartown and the summer team. The girls rode ponies to North Beach, likely along Starbuck Neck.

On leaving the island, the Edgars took the stagecoach from Edgartown to Cottage City, the Uncatena steamship to New Bedford then a trolley to Fall River. They reached Newport and rode the Puritan, another vessel, home to Jersey City.

In the 1960s, Louise became involved in the civil rights movement by supporting the Montgomery, Alabama bus boycott. She died in 1992 at the age of 101.[67]

CROQUET DOMINATED SOCIAL ACTIVITIES on Martha's Vineyard since the 1860s. Late in the century, some people wanted to make croquet more scientific, less a game of chance. The game of Roque was devised, using the rudiments of croquet. "The result was the birth of Roque, in which the wickets were narrowed, the courts made hard and smooth, and borders provided against which balls could be caused to carom."[68] Roque became quite popular.

Roque was popularized across the country and characterized as "croquet with a college education." The Roque ball was 3.25 inches in diameter, wickets set in the clay were 3.50 inches wide and the mallet was short and heavy. The hard clay court was framed with sturdy wooden timbers to encourage players to ricochet the ball and make it carom off the sideboards. As one guide explained, the game is "equal to billiards so far as skill, careful playing and head work are concerned."

Roque replaced croquet as a competitive sport in the summer Olympics, held in St. Louis, Missouri, in 1904. Four Americans competed, and the gold medal went to leading Roque advocate Charles Jacobus (age sixty-four), who had written the Spaulding Official Roque Guide. While including Roque in the Olympics added medals to those earned by the United

The game of roque, a scientific version of croquet, was popular around 1900. Courtesy of the Martha's Vineyard Museum.

The roque courts at Waban Park proved popular with all ages. Tennis and baseball also shared the field. Courtesy of the Martha's Vineyard Museum.

States, Roque, like croquet before it, was dropped from the London games, held in 1908.

In 1935, the fifty-fourth annual tournament was held for the Martha's Vineyard Roque Club, which maintained a membership log over the years. Eight courts were open at Waban Park, and it was played in the campground adjacent to Roque Avenue.

Another popular activity that tourists enjoyed was bowling. Two bowling alleys were in operation over the years in downtown Oak Bluffs, and it was not uncommon for young boys to earn a few pennies as pin setters. (Ball return was not invented until 1951.) With bowling alleys next to each other on Lake Avenue, bowlers were guaranteed the opportunity to roll for a strike for fun if not money.

AFTER THE TURN OF the century, a new group of visitors, comparable to the prominent wealthy elite of the 1880s, considered Martha's Vineyard a site for a private outpost to savor the out-of-doors without having to contend with the hoi polloi. The island became a site where the rich and famous could hobnob and savor their high-end lifestyle. No longer was the island a haven solely for middle-class Americans.

The Boston Herald of 1895 hailed the Vineyard as "one of the best fishing grounds on the New England coast," noting that mackerel, bluefish and swordfish were caught in great quantity. By 1912, the Gazette homed in on the quaint atmosphere of Vineyard Haven, a haven for fishermen and Vineyard sailors at home in a village nestled by the head of the harbor.

Sportsmen descended on the Vineyard to socialize, hunt or fish and to savor the rustic nature of Martha's Vineyard. These were upper-class tourists, vacationers who could make their influence felt with their prominence in politics, journalism or, most conveniently, financial stature. Many tycoons from Boston rode the dude train to Woods Hole. Martha's Vineyard became a refuge for those who sought a noble excuse to avoid the crowds and be among their social set. Such were the fishing and hunting clubs of the early 1900s.

Businessmen with deep pockets established private hunting clubs on the Vineyard in the early years of the twentieth century. The clubs were set up along the Vineyard's south shore, which was uninhabited, wild and untamed. The Watcha Club on Scrubby Neck was formed in 1903. This was followed by the Tisbury Pond Club, established in 1912 at Long Point with the purchase of 470 acres of woods and fields along the south shore. For several years, from 1912 to 1919, club members maintained a journal of their hunting prowess, which included listing their prey as well as current weather conditions. Their most successful year was 1914, when they shot 423 birds.

Local islanders maintained decoys and blinds for the hunters of the Tisbury Pond Club. "Social distinctions were more obvious and accepted when the Vineyard first came into its own as a vacation retreat from the city. But there was an obvious affection and friendship between the club members and the islanders they depended on for their needs."[69]

"Chris Kennedy of TTOR, [the Trustees of Reservation] island's regional director, said many people do not realize that sportsmen were some of the country's first conservationists." It is generally accepted that "without the generosity and vision of the club members it is unlikely the property would exist as it does today." To protect this land, descendants of

Hunting and fishing inspired wealthy sportsmen to build camps along the south shore. Three hunters, Hal Tripp, Chris Clark and H.P. Ayer, display their prowess. Courtesy of the Connie Sanborn collection.

the original Pond Club members donated their grounds to the Trustees of Reservation in 1977.[70]

In 1904, Elmer Bliss founded the Edgartown Yacht Club, a successor to the Home Club, a social group that held sailing regattas and encouraged yachting. Bliss was a "half-way summer visitor of the new era" and a grandson of whaling captain Jared Fisher. Renovations to Osborn's Wharf by Bliss, in 1928, provided a base of operations for the burgeoning summer sailing community, and the accompanying clubhouse "marked, in retrospect, the symbolic turning point of Edgartown's transformation into a summer resort." Elmer Bliss was named commodore of the Edgartown Yacht Club in 1927. The Vineyard Haven Yacht Club opened the next year, 1928.[71]

The Vineyard Sound Interclub–Class Sloop was designed in 1928, specifically to provide a class of sailboats where sailors competed on an equal footing with the yacht clubs of Edgartown, Vineyard Haven and Nantucket. This class of sailboat was popular from the 1920s to the 1950s. The Edgartown Regatta welcomed cruising sailing vessels and racing yachts. "It became an increasingly popular annual event, introducing recreational sailors from up and down the East Coast to Edgartown." The regatta began in 1924.[72]

Yacht clubs became an integral aspect in the lifestyle of the nouveaux riche, just as the New York Yacht Club had been an elite group in previous years, gathering at the Oak Bluffs Club. Joy's Pier in Oak Bluffs was another center of boat traffic, although much less ostentatious.

Golf and tennis gained popularity as sports of the well-to-do. The first golf course was laid out near the West Chop lighthouse in 1893; it consisted of six holes. A nine-hole course in the Highlands became the East Chop Club in 1910. The first Edgartown golf course was laid out in 1897 but not officially opened until 1926. Vineyard Haven golf was planned in 1898, and Mink Meadows opened in 1928. New activities catered to the wealthy lifestyle. The Oak Bluffs Country Club boasted, "The climate of the island is delightful—very even, and neither too hot nor too cold."

Ed Mulligan laid out a golf course in Oak Bluffs but could not complete the project, as he was involved in an auto accident when his car frightened a horse, which threw a farmer, who died, in Vineyard Haven. Mulligan was accused of speeding in 1902, and the town selectmen responded by setting the speed limit at six miles per hour in town. Another man, Lyman Besse, completed the golf course but not until 1910. This became the Island Golf Club and, in 1979, morphed into Farm Neck.

What had been an Oak Bluffs sheep pasture became the East Chop Country Club and later the East Chop Tennis Club. Lawn tennis was played at Waban Park on eight clay courts that had to be rolled, holes filled and tape laid down every day. Cost to play was eight dollars per week.

Horse racing proved an unlikely activity. Locals made the most of the horse racing, and off-islanders were invited to bet their money. The half-mile track at Girdlestone Park continued into the twentieth century—more than thirty years. Tickets were ten dollars per season, and first prize was fifty dollars.

Along Barnes Road, south of the roundabout between the two Deer Run entrances, the foundations of the bleachers of Girdlestone Park nestle in the underbrush. The oval track was laid out in an open field and is visible to this day. The track at Girdlestone was not designed for saddle horse racing "but rather two-wheeled 'sulky races' which drew both horse enthusiasts and gamblers to these popular events." Advertisements in newspapers off-island bragged, "Lovers of the harness horse will see some very spirited racing during the season at Girdlestone Park at Martha's Vineyard."[73]

Around the same time, another racetrack, known as Whiting's Farm Trotting Park, located across from the West Tisbury cemetery on State Road, also drew horse enthusiasts.

Retired whaling captain George Fred Tilton recalled, "A bunch who were always racing for anything from a plug of tobacco to a sack of oats used to meet pretty regular." According to Tilton, "We induced quite a number of men to bring horses from the Cape and New Bedford to race at this track, Girdlestone, and Whiting's track at West Tisbury." Tilton continued, "Fast horses were brought to the Island and faster horses were bought by the Vineyard boys, so that we made a pretty good showing every time we turned out."

"Many sports have come and mostly gone from the Island—roque, polo, whaleboat racing, fox hunts, tricycling, and sulky racing among them. But one sport has outlasted them all: baseball." Often, there were pickup games in the late nineteenth century, with players from Tisbury, Edgartown and the Martha's Vineyard Herald of Cottage City. And tourists flocked to watch these games, supporting their teams.[74]

Favorite fields were Tashmoo Park overlooking Lake Tashmoo and Ocean Park in Cottage City, "but it was soon eclipsed in popularity by a nearby field: Waban Park, now Alley Park," where more professional games were played. "This was a serious, professional team, built from some of the best college players in New England, almost entirely off-Islanders."

By the turn of the century, baseball proved a popular spectator sport at Waban Park in Cottage City. Courtesy of the Connie Sanborn collection.

George Wright played a couple of seasons for the Cottage Citys then went on to a stellar career with the Cincinnati Red Stockings, followed by the Boston Red Stockings. George Wright was considered the best shortstop of the era. His elder brother, Harry, was the team manager and the Wright brothers were both inducted into the Baseball Hall of Fame.

"On the Vineyard, an upstart baseball league made up of town teams and players was flourishing. The league is believed to have started in the early 1900s, although reports differ whether the teams were made up of professionals, Islanders or a combination of both."

"The most famous baseball player to ever swing a bat on the Vineyard was Pie Traynor, generally considered the greatest National League third baseman prior to the 1950s." Traynor played with the Pittsburgh Pirates from 1920 to 1937. In the 1927 World Series, he played against Babe Ruth and Lou Gehrig. He is the only Cape Cod League player inducted into the hall of fame. According to old box scores, "In the summer of 1919, at the age of 20, Mr. Traynor spent half his summer playing for the Oak Bluffs town team, while spending the rest of his time on the Cape playing for Falmouth." He hit .265 for Oak Bluffs that summer. The league was made up of both professionals and amateurs.

Another game of renown, decades later, was up-island in the field of dreams. "Over the course of eight decades, the Chilmark game has woven its own rich tapestry of memories that now rivals the greater history of baseball on the Island." Aside from appearances in this summer Sunday softball series by Roger Baldwin and Spike Lee, "the most noteworthy visit came from an iconic figure who connected the history of both Vineyard baseball and the national pastime." Famed second baseman Jackie Robinson was called to pinch-hit in a Chilmark game in 1972. Actually, he attended as a friend of the late photojournalist Peter Simon, and Simon offered to let him pinch-hit, but Robinson declined. It was a moment in time that is still treasured by those in attendance that day, all those years ago.[75]

Basketball offered exciting entertainment for the down-island winter community from the 1920s until 1959. And while the sport did not involve tourists from off-island, as it was a winter sport, the reputation of town team competition engendered by the games enticed off-islanders to appreciate the Vineyard even more in season.

James Naismith invented basketball at the Springfield YMCA in 1891. He sought an indoor activity and used peach baskets attached ten feet off the gym floor as a target to throw a soccer ball. Those were the rudiments of the early game.

In 1906, the first game was played on the Vineyard between Tisbury and Oak Bluffs, according to retired high school coach Jay Schofield. Edgartown joined in 1925. It was a rough game in the early years.

Edgartown originally played above the town hall on Main Street, until the town built a new school with a gymnasium that held two hundred people. Tisbury played above the town hall before the new school (still in use) was built in 1929 and accommodated a crowd of five hundred. Oak Bluffs first played in the old fire station, then at Noepe Hall over Dreamland garage before it built a gym in 1952.

Basketball depended on the two-handed shot; one-handed was deemed inaccurate and only used in layups. Fouls were thrown underhand with two hands. A player's height determined the position they played.

In 1927, the principals of the three high schools organized a league where the schools competed to be the Vineyard Champion. Before each game, the team would play the alumni. As many as forty games per season were played between the schools of Edgartown, Oak Bluffs and Tisbury.

Girls' basketball was less physical and slower. Oak Bluffs girls won the Lions Club Cup in 1936. Junior high students started to play in a league as well.

This community off-season activity encouraged hero worship among the "basketeers." A typical audience was one-third students and two-thirds local townspeople and parents.

Over the years, student skills improved, coaching got better and changes in the shooting technique increased scoring. An average team in the 1930s scored twenty-two points per game; by the late 1940s, it rose to thirty-seven; and by the 1950s, an average score was sixty-two. In 1941, Edgartown won an off-island tournament and was met at the ferry slip with cheering crowds and fire trucks with lights flashing and sirens wailing.

George Santos Sr. played on the '42 Tisbury team. He said, "Each school had its turn at winning." He was an expert on Vineyard basketball history. The popularity of the game was based on the island insularity, the proximity of the towns and intense local pride.[76]

The program ended in 1959, when the island school system was regionalized.

At the age of twenty, Vineyarder Bayes Norton (1903–1967) of Vineyard Haven participated in the 1924 summer Olympics. Norton made his name at Phillips Exeter then Yale and became an Olympic sprinter.

He sailed aboard the steamship America to Paris. Norton finished second in the 200-meter race at the U.S. Olympic trials and fifth at the Olympic Games of 1924. Norton was the father of Jim Norton of Bayes Norton farms on the Vineyard Haven/Oak Bluffs town line.[77]

After the turn of the century, even the Civil War statue faced a change. The purpose of the statue was to ease tensions caused by the Civil War. (The statue had water troughs on its base for horses to drink.) Dedicated in 1891, the statue was established in its prominent place at Farland Square by the base of Circuit Avenue. In 1930, it was moved to make way for a traffic light. The new location was on the edge of Ocean Park, facing the ocean to welcome tourists and visitors. The statue was rededicated in 1931, with the original benefactor, editor Charles Strahan of the Cottage City Star, once more in attendance.

After the excitement engendered by the amusement park atmosphere in Oak Bluffs, Martha's Vineyard settled into a state of somnolence for nearly a half century—first World War I and then Prohibition, followed by the Great Depression and World War II. Tourists did visit the Vineyard on occasion and sought houses to rent. The Lazy Days booklets of the late 1920s listed numerous houses available, noting, "All houses furnished complete except linen and silver." Visitors were welcome, though they were in short supply.

During World War I, the local highlight was a visit from Massachusetts lieutenant governor Calvin Coolidge and governor Samuel McCall in 1918, honoring residents of Gay Head who volunteered for military service in the highest percentage of enlistees of any Massachusetts town.

Economically, the Vineyard struggled. Tourism fell off with the onset of war. The first airplane arrived as the trolley service shut down at the end of World War I. Prohibition opened the door for other activities that did less to encourage tourists to visit the Vineyard, such as rumrunning. Martha's Vineyard felt the impact imposed by Prohibition on the legality of alcohol. The Great Depression added to the sense of gloom and despair.

The Capawok movie theater opened in Vineyard Haven in 1913. (The recently renovated Capawok is a fixture of the summer film scene.) In Oak Bluffs, two theaters opened, and today, the Strand, like the Capawok, has been refurbished and stands proudly awaiting summer moviegoers. The

Island Theatre on Circuit Avenue still stands, barely. It has not screened a film in years. On rainy days, or for matinees, tourists with time on their hands could find refuge in a movie theater. As more movies were released, theaters became a standard but sedentary form of recreation—the participant did not have to move, as all the action moved across the screen.

From movie theaters to baseball games, tourists appreciated the Vineyard at various levels of activity. The scenic sites still prevailed but were supplemented by amusements that stimulated tourists in new directions. Additionally, the ability to travel by jitney or motorcar opened more scenes and activities for tourists to explore beyond the cliffs of Gay Head and South Beach and allowed families and friends to plan individualized recreational events and more varied vacations.

African American Tourism (1890–1950)

Martha's Vineyard, one of New England's finest summer resorts.[78]
—Martha's Vineyard Island Via New Haven Railroad

T ourism on Martha's Vineyard was not limited to the white population. African Americans were inspired to visit the Vineyard and made it a refuge to which they returned year after year. The Vineyard was color-blind in making tourist activities accessible.

There were slaves on Martha's Vineyard in the eighteenth century. The census of 1765 counted forty-six black people on the Vineyard, which probably included free blacks as well as slaves. Quock Walker, a slave, won his freedom in a court case in 1783. That elevated Massachusetts to a unique position on the abolition of slavery. Massachusetts became the first state to allow slaves to petition the court for their freedom, which propelled Massachusetts to the realm of an abolitionist haven and allowed the state to accept runaway slaves.

On Martha's Vineyard, several incidents unfolded that were indicative of the abolitionist sentiments akin to activities on the Underground Railroad.

Initially, free blacks came to Martha's Vineyard to work as laborers, sailors, craftsmen and often whalemen. As an island, the Vineyard attracted free slaves to work on whaleships and in the fishing industry. Local people sold land to black residents. The first federal census of 1790 listed thirty-nine blacks on the Vineyard. The black population on Martha's Vineyard averaged between 4 percent and 5 percent, or about two hundred people in the early 1800s.

Toward the end of the eighteenth century, the Wampanoag were marginalized into three areas on the Vineyard: Chappaquiddick, Gay Head and Christiantown. Intermarriages occurred between African Americans and Native Americans, especially in the Gay Head community.

White residents of Martha's Vineyard and those of other New England communities signed petitions advocating to free all the slaves nationwide. These petitions were prepared in the 1830s and duly sent to Congress to advocate abolition legislation. However, since most signers were women, they were not accepted because women could not vote. That denial initiated an alliance between women suffrage and emancipation.

Few African Americans attended Camp Meeting in the early years. However, two prominent African Americans were selected as preachers and exhorted the crowds of Wesleyan Grove. Father John Wright preached in the campground in 1856 and raised money for his Ohio college. Henson, the model for Uncle Tom also spoke before the gathering in 1858.

The Camp Meeting community professed abolition, but blacks neither bought nor built in the campground in the nineteenth century, although the owners of Thayer cottage did host a number of black visitors.

Adelaide Cromwell researched and wrote extensively on the history of African Americans in resort communities along the Eastern Seaboard. She discovered a pattern of settlement that proved similar, regardless of which summer vacation destination she reviewed.

Initially, a few African Americans came to the community seeking year-round work. They journeyed to where the jobs were, whether as a day laborer, a long-term sailor, craftsman or journeyman. Once a small black settlement was underway, parishioners built a church. That came first. Often a school followed. The challenge in a resort community was that there are generally two employment seasons, winter and summer, so jobs were plentiful in the summer but scarce in the off-season.

Second, in the summer months, a number of black people came with the intent to work for affluent white vacationers, cleaning, cooking or washing clothes. Other blacks established guesthouses or small rooming houses, acknowledging the segregated restrictions on housing with entrenched racism. Still, wealthy blacks often prevailed, establishing a precedent that enabled more blacks to visit vacation resort communities.

Third, a few middle-class blacks chose to vacation and stayed in black-owned guesthouses in a resort community. Later, many of these people bought their own houses in the area. This pattern was followed in numerous black resort communities along the coast, and we see it in detail on Martha's Vineyard. "The black resort at Oak Bluffs is extremely popular and it illustrates by its history and social structure the complexities and the changes in black resort lifestyles."[79]

Following the Civil War, a number of white families traveled to the Vineyard with their black servants. The servants appreciated the opportunity to summer on the Vineyard, even though they had to work. "Blacks, too, as soon as they could afford it, followed paths similar to those of comparable Whites and sought convenient watering spots."[80]

In her piece on black history on Martha's Vineyard, Anne G. Morgan wrote, "The surge in vacationers also brought African-Americans who came not to play, but to work—as nannies, drivers, and cooks. Soon, this group formed their own subset of the community and started an organization of domestic workers, the Open Door Club."[81]

Blacks purchased property on the Vineyard, primarily in Oak Bluffs, as Jim Crow prejudice was evident across the rest of the Vineyard. In the early years of the twentieth century, about thirty black people owned homes in Oak Bluffs. And Oak Bluffs was said to be the largest black resort on the East Coast between 1900 and 1930.

Shearer Cottage has welcomed guests for over a century. The inn was a hallmark of the African American community in the Highlands. Courtesy of Joyce Dresser.

Mrs. Anthony Smith, who lived in Boston, bought a house in the campground but was pressured to actually move her house out onto Circuit Avenue. Mrs. Smith was black, and blacks were not accepted in the campground. The houses in the campground were erected on tent platforms, which were easily hauled by a team of oxen. Mrs. Smith's boardinghouse had an annex on Pocasset Street.

In 1899, Louisa Izett and her sister, Georgia O'Brien, opened the Tivoli Inn on Circuit Avenue, adjacent to Mrs. Smith's boardinghouse, overlooking Hiawatha Park. The Tivoli Inn catered to those people of color who were denied access to white-only hotels and offered their guests inexpensive rooms. The inn was promoted to tourists and workers who needed a short-term place to stay.

These boardinghouses were the progenitor of Shearer Cottage, a significant hostelry that opened in Oak Bluffs, specifically for blacks, shortly after the turn of the century.

In 1903, Charles and Henrietta Shearer bought a summer house in the Highlands. They were Baptists and sought to be near the Baptist tabernacle. Henrietta opened a laundry service for white families.

Charles Shearer was a former slave, who graduated from Hampton Institute and worked at the Parker House in Boston. The Shearers encountered a typical Vineyard experience: off-island friends and family invited themselves to visit, and the Shearers were confounded on what to do. They expanded their property and, in 1912, opened their house as Shearer Cottage, an inn dedicated to African American visitors.

It was a brilliant move. Shearer Cottage, a hotel for African Americans, is situated near the circle of the Baptist tabernacle in the Highlands of Oak Bluffs. It was an immediate hit. Black tourists appreciated that the hotel served meals and provided clean, personalized guest rooms. Local people appreciated the ready source of employment, which ranged from cooking, cleaning or working in the laundry to waiting tables in the dining room. Many visitors met their spouse there, which made Shearer an idyllic matchmaker. Often, couples bought property in the Highlands because Shearer had established a welcome site for them.

Boston blacks began to come to the Vineyard around 1900, and Shearer Cottage was often their destination. Over the years, luminaries of the African American community spent time at Shearer, including Adam Clayton Powell Jr., Ethel Waters, Paul Robeson and Harry T. Burleigh. More recently, Lionel Richie and the Commodores stayed at Shearer for a wedding. The cottage became a social center of the black community in Oak Bluffs. Descendants of the Shearer family still run the cottage today. And artifacts from the cottage were donated to the National Museum of African American History and Culture in Washington, D.C.

Shearer Cottage was a boon for the African American summer visitor. Its presence solidified the opportunity for blacks to savor the seaside options of Oak Bluffs. Today, both the Tivoli Inn and Shearer Cottage continue to offer lodging for tourists and are often sought after by people whose traditions were laid down more than a century ago.

Aside from the success of Charles Shearer and Shearer Cottage, a second personality emerged to enlarge the stature of the African American population and attract black tourists from off-island to visit the Vineyard. Between 1900 and World War II, this effort succeeded in merging the year-round population with the summer people—two disparate cohorts. A local church accomplished this.

This local church was established to inculcate and educate immigrants on Martha's Vineyard. The Oakland Mission, founded by Susan Bradley, was dedicated to teach English and assimilate immigrants into the cultural aspects of mainstream America. Bradley had established the mission to acculturate Portuguese immigrants, primarily from the Azores and Cape Verdean Islands.

Reverend Oscar Denniston emigrated from Jamaica in 1900 to work with Susan Bradley at the mission. After Bradley's death in 1907, Denniston assumed management of the mission and renamed it the Bradley Memorial Mission. He expanded services and welcomed the black community of Martha's Vineyard and beyond.

Bradley Mission drew parishioners from across the Vineyard because it welcomed blacks, whites, Native Americans and immigrants from the Azores and the Cape Verdean Islands. Reverend Denniston served the Bradley Mission more than forty years, turning it into a central force in the black community. He encouraged everyone to come to his church located right off Circuit Avenue.

Oscar Denniston had three children with his first wife, Charlotte, who died in 1905. He traveled back to Jamaica and returned to the Vineyard with a second wife, Medora, with whom he had five more children. All the Denniston children went to college; at one time, four siblings were attending Boston University at the same time. Several settled in Oak Bluffs and always had a warm spot for their youth, growing up part of a bustling, exciting community.

By 1920, about 175 blacks lived in Dukes County—the majority in Oak Bluffs. Through the influence of Shearer Cottage and the Bradley Memorial Mission, the summer and year-round communities merged as they incorporated social connections through the cottage and the mission, which solidified the black community on the island.

WILLIAM TROTTER, EDITOR OF the Boston Guardian, a black paper, wrote in 1933 of black visitors from Boston, who enjoyed the charm and camaraderie of Shearer Cottage and the religious and social leadership of Reverend Denniston. More affluent blacks chose to summer in Oak Bluffs. And while blacks did own homes in several Vineyard towns, the heart of the African American community was in the Highlands—the Baptist Highlands—in Oak Bluffs.

Blacks visited the Vineyard from Boston, New Bedford, Springfield and Worcester, Massachusetts, and Providence, Rhode Island. Back home, they were friends and socialized when on island. Groups from Boston were among the most cohesive. "Most had ties already forged in the Boston area. There was no social hierarchy within this group. They were a community of equals, transplanted friends, a group of about forty." In many cases, when the family had purchased a summer home, the wife and children summered on-island, while the husbands commuted on weekends. In the Highlands, more than a dozen cottages were owned by Bostonians "The lifestyle was simple, warm and relaxed. Recreation was bathing at High Beach, playing tennis and cards and visiting with friends. The same people came year after year."[82] (High Beach refers to the beach by the Highland Pier, now by the East Chop Beach Club.)

Following rave reviews and word of mouth from two New Yorkers, spiritualist Harry Burleigh and Harlem politician Adam Clayton Powell, New York tourists and vacationers flocked to the Vineyard. Doctors, lawyers, businessmen, teachers and other civil servants followed. The Vineyard became a place to form friendships, see and be seen, savor the scenic atmosphere and enjoy the beaches.

Jill Nelson, author of Finding Martha's Vineyard, recalled Dorothy West, a product of the Harlem Renaissance and a productive writer. "It wasn't till I was almost grown and had known her for years and years as the tiny, birdlike woman with the thick Boston accent who talked faster than seemed humanly possible, whom I often saw around town, at the post office and occasionally on my mother's porch, that I realized this friendly, talkative neighbor was also the famous writer Dorothy West."[83]

"Ms. West, a longtime resident of the Vineyard, described the growth of that summer community in a 1971 Gazette article. 'Probably 12 cottages—all Bostonians…neither arrogant nor obsequious, they neither overacted or played ostrich…they were 'cool'—a common condition of black Bostonians.'"[84]

The 1971 Gazette article on the summer community in the Highlands continued, capturing the words of Dorothy West:

> For some years the black Bostonians, growing in modest numbers, had this idyll to themselves. And then came the black New Yorkers.…
>
> And then came the black New Yorkers. They had heard of a fair land whose equality was a working phrase. They joyously tested it. They behaved like New Yorkers because they were not Bostonians. There is nobody like a Bostonian except a man who is one.
>
> The New Yorkers did not talk in low voices. They talked in happy voices. They carried baskets of food to the beach to make the day last. They carried liquor of the best brands. They grouped together in an ever increasing circle because what was the sense of sitting apart. Their women wore diamonds, when the few Bostonians who owned any had left theirs at home. They wore paint and powder when in Boston only a sporting woman bedecked her face in such bold attire. Their dresses were cut low. They wore high heels on sandy roads.[85]

Thus the Highlands incorporated middle-class blacks of both the Boston and New York communities, attracted by friends or word of mouth. Some met their spouses at Shearer Cottage. Often, they returned, purchased a summer cottage and became part of the summer community in Oak Bluffs. Later, many found employment and discovered that they could enjoy the Vineyard year-round. Others returned in their retirement to a place where all nationalities and races are accepted, the pace is slower and the vistas are always enchanting.

DURING WORLD WAR II, Adelaide Cromwell, a cousin to Senator Edward Brooke, was not alone in seeking out the Vineyard for a summer home. Dr. Cromwell, born in 1919 in Washington, D.C., earned her doctorate in sociology from Radcliffe Institute and served at Boston University as a professor of sociology from 1951 to 1985. She was instrumental in development of BU's African Studies program. Dr. Cromwell passed away in 2019.

Dr. Cromwell's seminal work was The Other Brahmins, a study of the social caste system and role of race over two hundred years. Dr. Cromwell wrote of Boston blacks who exhibited social leadership skills that impacted their political and economic worlds. Her primary conceit compared upper-class black and white women in the era of World War II. The book focuses on the sociological impact of northern women in the class system.

As noted, a key element of Dr. Cromwell's research in the settlement of a black summer resort community unfolded on Martha's Vineyard, specifically in Oak Bluffs. "Blacks, too, as soon as they could afford it, followed paths similar to those of comparable Whites and sought convenient watering spots." Cromwell continued her review of the black resort that developed in Oak Bluffs, noting by its history how it reflected the structures and struggles of resort lifestyles for African Americans. And she recognized the popularity of the Highlands.

In an article for his weekly Oak Bluffs column, Skip Finley shared a conversation he had with Adelaide Cromwell in 2014. "She is delighted about the news that Oak Bluffs is to be acknowledged by the Smithsonian. She told me that it was called Cottage City when her aunt bought her house, where Dr. Cromwell stayed when she first visited, and I laughed saying that was indeed the point."[86]

"HISTORICALLY BLACK BEACH COMMUNITIES date back as far as the 1930s in a handful of coastal areas across the United States. Many sprang up during segregation when blacks were either barred from whites-only beaches or simply unwelcome." A majority of summer resorts for blacks were located in the South, but a number of popular sites arose in the Northeast.[87]

In the early 1900s, middle-class black Americans faced discrimination in housing at beach resort areas or had to make do in segregated communities. While many of these middle-class blacks were well off, because of discriminatory strictures, they were denied access to resort hotels and restaurants in popular resort communities. There was discrimination in Oak Bluffs, as well as other resort communities that catered to the black population.

Sites along the East Coast that welcomed blacks included Highland Beach on the Chesapeake Bay; Cape May, New Jersey; and Sag Harbor, New York. On Long Island, the Hamptons, Sag Harbor Hills, Ninevah Beach and Azurest were unique among coastal communities. African Americans populated the area for decades, enjoying a separate scenic locale from whites. Segregation was the social status quo everywhere in the early twentieth century.

And while segregation per se has been overcome to a great degree, racial parity is still a challenge. Highland Beach is a historic black resort near Annapolis, Maryland. Prominent blacks, such as Langston Hughes, Paul Robeson and Booker T. Washington summered there. South Carolina's rural Sea Islands are vacation sites populated by the Gullah community, descendants of slaves who speak a language part African part English.

Today, these beachfront communities are facing challenges beyond their borders. For years, most historically black compounds along the shores have been immune from property development and real estate price escalation. However, since 2000, that has changed. Choice beachfront acreage has become a prime market for investors who want to build more and larger houses and sell the properties to upscale buyers, regardless of race. House prices have risen dramatically as the vacation community has been driven up by demand.

"As values soar in surrounding locations, pricing out many second-home buyers, historically black beach enclaves from American Beach near Jacksonville, Florida, to South Carolina's rural Sea Islands are seeing sharp increases in development and new home buyers." Prime ocean sites are now a valuable commodity and have "increased in value with the development of expansive expensive summer communities. And along the Chesapeake, once havens for African-American life and culture are now prized as potential sites of commercialization." Naturally, this has had a negative impact on black second-home ownership.[88]

Remarkably, while Oak Bluffs reflects aspects of other black resort communities, with an even longer history than most, the town has not suffered to the same degree. There are still instances of discrimination in New England resorts, yet blacks found solace where they could enjoy a peaceful, safe setting. Shearer Cottage proved to be such a site.

Another perspective is offered on the history of black beach communities: "Oak Bluffs, a sliver of Martha's Vineyard that is home to a lively African-American population, has long attracted wealthy second-home buyers. But the town holds a unique history for African-Americans."[89]

Richard Taylor is the author of Martha's Vineyard: Race, Property, and the Power of Place. Taylor is the director of the Center for Real Estate at Boston's Suffolk University. On the Vineyard, he contends that restrictions on development have limited construction of properties close to the ocean, affecting both blacks and whites. While the Vineyard has a beautiful shoreline, house construction has been monitored and controlled so that rampant price increases have not disrupted vacationing middle- and upper-class black Americans.

Oak Bluffs is fortunate in that it represents a unique site for African Americans. Martha's Vineyard continues to be a center of activity and action for the black community, attracting nationally known leaders from Spike Lee to Skip Gates. The town is a prime site for black homeowners. "'We have film festivals and book clubs and churches all dedicated to the history and culture of African-American life,' says Taylor, who has owned a home in the East Chop section of Oak Bluffs since the 1970s."[90]

HISTORICALLY, MARTHA'S VINEYARD BLACKS, former slaves or freedmen, were drawn to the island as local laborers or to work in the fishing and whaling industries. They purchased property on-island and formed the nascent black community.

Toward the end of the nineteenth century, middle-class blacks visited the Vineyard, staying at Shearer Cottage, the Tivoli Inn or Villa Rosa. Many purchased property in the Highlands or elsewhere in Oak Bluffs. Dorothy West, a Harlem Renaissance writer and author of The Wedding, bought property in the Highlands in 1948 and never looked back.

The town became accepted and appreciated as a welcome haven for notable personalities in the civil rights movement. In the 1960s, Harlem labor organizer and politician Joseph Overton invited prominent blacks to vacation at his summer home across from the Inkwell on Sea View Avenue in Oak Bluffs. Men such as Joe Louis, Harry Belafonte, Malcolm X, Jesse Jackson, Ralph Abernathy and Dr. Martin Luther King Jr. chose to spend peaceful vacation days by the ocean's shores in the welcoming community offered at Villa Rosa. President Barack Obama vacationed on the Vineyard seven out of his eight years as president after discovering the Vineyard while still an Illinois senator. And in 2019, the Obamas purchased a twenty-nine-acre estate on Edgartown Great Pond for $12 million.[91]

What was once known as the Gold Coast ran from Circuit Avenue to Vineyard Sound and from Tuckernuck to Ocean Park in downtown Oak Bluffs. As more people bought houses in town, the result was more parties, more social gatherings and more enjoyment of participation in the beachfront community.

The most central meeting place of the black community in Oak Bluffs is Town Beach, known as the Inkwell. The name may have been drawn from members of the Harlem Renaissance and the Amsterdam News, a prominent Harlem newspaper. The writers found inspiration in the swirling, dashing waters that washed onto the idyllic beach, reminiscent of ink flowing in an inkwell. Another provenance for the name was from author Dorothy West, who mentored children at the beach, meeting at the Inkwell. While the beach was historically the sign of segregation, today it stands as a symbol of unity, harmony and integration of the races.

For decades, the Inkwell has been the hub of summer activity, hosted by the Polar Bears, a loosely affiliated group of vacationers who savor swimming in the delightful ocean waters. The first Polar Bear dips in the water on Memorial Day and the last leaves by Columbus Day. Besides swimming, the Polar Bears share the social delights of their neighbors, friends and family with exercising, singing and sharing potluck meals.

Oak Bluffs earned a reputation as a delightful vacation site for blacks from across the country. Families travel hundreds of miles to savor the unique charm and historic ambiance of the black resort community of Oak Bluffs. Other Vineyard towns did not garner as much admiration from the black community, due to unwritten mores on segregation in property purchase and even hotel reservations.

The Inkwell Beach was initially segregated. Today it is a symbol of diversity and inclusion in Oak Bluffs and the Vineyard. Courtesy of Joyce Dresser.

Generations of black travelers who had to deal with the fear and trauma of discrimination depended on The Negro Motorist Green Book, a guidebook that listed restaurants, hotels and other businesses that welcomed black patrons. Hotels, restaurants and gas stations are integral to travelers, and a Green Book endorsement ensured a quality establishment catered to black families. From the Maine coast to New York State and all through the South, Victor Green's guide was a staple for black automobile travelers, from its inception in 1936 until the civil rights movement made it superfluous, or almost so, in 1966. In 1956, the Green Book listed eight cottages in Oak Bluffs that welcomed black guests.[92]

Shortly after World War II, Ebony magazine promoted the Vineyard as a vacation site that welcomed members of the African American community. Other magazines have promoted the Vineyard over the years, but it was the 1947 issue of Ebony that had the most lasting impact. From Ebony, "Negro and white swim together on the public beaches, rub shoulders at public affairs."

Ebony wrote, "[The] most exclusive Negro summer colony in the country is at quaint historical Oak Bluffs on Martha's Vineyard….Between negro and white residents, a quiet competition has developed in the improvement of homes. Negroes know their property is being watched by white neighbors. The result is that the Negro summer colony on Oak Bluffs is as modern and inviting as any middle class summer resort in the country."[93]

LOOKING BACK OVER HER long life, Adelaide Cromwell concluded that "by the mid-fifties, Oak Bluffs was a heterogeneous black resort with summer visitors coming from all over the country and abroad."[94]

Anne Morgan wrote, "The African-American elite who summer on the Vineyard, as well as increased references in popular culture, such as the 1994 film The Inkwell, have increased the island's prominence and popularity. As the African-American community has grown, it has expanded beyond Oak Bluffs." Morgan added, "Spurred by the economic prosperity that followed World War II, African-Americans flocked to Oak Bluffs to buy and rent summer homes." These words were included in a play set on Martha's Vineyard, titled Continuing the Tradition: African Americans on Martha's Vineyard for Stick Fly. It was produced at the Huntington Theatre in Boston.

On segregation, there is a sense that it is part of the past. "Many African-Americans here, year-rounders and summer visitors alike, insist it is not segregated. 'This is one of the most integrated communities, racially and economically, that there is,' said Vernon Jordan, the lawyer and former civil rights leader, who has rented a summer place for years." Jordan's wife, Ann, vacationed on the Vineyard as a child, as did her cousin Valerie Jarrett, advisor and friend to President Obama.

"We'd hitchhike all over the island," Ms. Jarrett said. "I never experienced a hint of discrimination on the island in more than 40 years."[95] That Senator Edward Brooke chose to spend his vacation time on Martha's Vineyard made a positive impact on the island in the 1950s and 1960s. Brooke was the first African American elected to the Senate since Reconstruction. Initially he came to the Vineyard as a tourist after he served in the segregated forces during World War II. Brooke bought property in Oak Bluffs in 1958 and formed a social organization, the Oak Bluffs Club. During his two terms as a United States senator, Mr. Brooke enjoyed his vacation retreat on the Vineyard and continued for decades afterwards as a summer fixture in Oak Bluffs.

The Cottagers, a social advocacy philanthropic group, was established in 1956 "to do good works in the community and to provide fellowship for the children of members." Its annual house tour and fashion show are spectacular fundraisers, drawing the African American community together

Senator Edward Brooke vacationed in Oak Bluffs more than half a century and became an icon of the community. Courtesy of the Connie Sanborn collection.

and welcoming tourists and locals alike. Limited to one hundred property owners—all black women—the Cottagers has put a positive public face on the Vineyard community.

Varied activities and programs emerged to entertain and amuse the summer population. Blacks were involved in games of tennis, bridge, poker, fishing and acting with the Shearer Summer Theatre. Five to Sevens were get-togethers with drinks, food and plenty of small talk, where the individual homes morphed into social gatherings. Art shows featured nationally known artist Lois Mailou Jones, and concerts included jazz pianist Eddie Haywood. And the beaches, especially the Inkwell, have drawn people for generations, as "most Blacks come to Oak Bluffs to enjoy the beach, if not the swimming." The Art Show at the Tabernacle has proved to be a popular activity over the years.[96]

When black summer tourists evolved into permanent prominent year-rounders in the 1950s, the Vineyard benefited. Rufus Shorter was named superintendent of schools in 1977. Herbert Tucker was appointed presiding judge in 1980. Both men signified the merging of summer and year-rounders and broadened the structure of the black community on Martha's Vineyard.

Many blacks return to the Vineyard each year. And a growing number come to buy a summer house or a second home or retire and move to Martha's Vineyard permanently. The increased diversity of the resort community has occurred as blacks who summered in Oak Bluffs coexist with the year-round black population. As Dr. Adelaide Cromwell wrote in 1984, "The Black presence, at first mostly in Oak Bluffs and now throughout the island, is permanent and promising." The tourist community, and the island as a whole, has benefitted from the continued presence of a robust African American tourist population.[97]

As a tourist community, Martha's Vineyard was dramatically interrupted by World War II. Life for both blacks and whites changed. More opportunities arose, but many traditions faltered and failed. The trajectory of the Vineyard as a mecca for tourism faced a challenge in the postwar era.

Post–World War II Tourism (1950–90)

Edgartown has no traffic lights or train or factory whistle.[98]
—Martha's Vineyard Chamber of Commerce Guide

According to the Vineyard Gazette of April 26, 1935, "Martha's Vineyard is still full of the qualities prominent in the panorama of the years, still unspoiled, still awaiting the visitor with recreations and delights in the summer sea."

By 1940, the Vineyard had become an outlier—a place so remote and removed that small-time crook Harold Tracy could escape from crimes committed in Kentucky, move to Oak Bluffs, murder a woman and never get caught. Dean Denniston, son of the reverend, observed that a murder on the Vineyard, while chilling and frightful, made the national press. He said that was good news, as it drew attention to the island.

And in 1942, aviator Charles Lindberg sought and found seclusion at Seven Gates in West Tisbury. He was able to avoid journalists who questioned his "America First" isolationism at the start of World War II. The Vineyard had faded from the center of attention and activity.

The postwar generation adapted to the new world order and gradually set the tone for a rise in the role tourism plays on the Vineyard today.

The Vineyard Gazette of May 9, 1952, described three types of tourists. The outsider considers Martha's Vineyard a marine park, an island out in the

Atlantic Ocean. The insider believes the Vineyard is paradisiac, like Heaven, where one can play golf six days out of seven, year-round—a second Florida. And then there's the realist, who complains that spring is cold and late—that the land is hilly like Vermont and craggy like the Scottish moors. Perhaps a bit of all that is true.

Martha's Vineyard gradually adjusted to the postwar world. Tourists still visited the Vineyard, but it was not a prime resort community. Servicemen stationed at the naval air station appreciated the island lifestyle, and many settled permanently on the Vineyard after their tour of service. Joseph Stiles was stationed on the Vineyard for three weeks before he realized he was on an island. He fell in love with a Cape Verdean woman, settled on the Vineyard and raised his family.

The 1950s and 1960s were not a great time for tourism on Martha's Vineyard. The island cultivated a reputation for being remote and removed—apart from the mainstream. The atmosphere was almost isolationist. If you lived on the Vineyard, fine, but who would want to go there? And why?

Residents made a living fishing or farming. The population was static. Tourists were looked upon not with distain but curiosity. Why would you want to come here? What do we have to offer?

Services on-island were minimal in the 1950s and early 1960s. Restaurants made their money off the small local crowd. Hotels were occasionally busy, but the tourist realm was limited. The year-round Vineyard population was approximately five thousand. A few tour buses lumbered along their appointed rounds each summer. And gift shop tchotchkes found their way into customers' handbags, but the overwhelming crowds and incessant, insistent traffic, was not (yet) part of mainstream lifestyle on the Vineyard.

Whilhelmina Lillian Chignell, "Chiggie," was on her way to vacation on Nantucket in the late 1890s, when inclement weather forced the steamship to land in Oak Bluffs. Undeterred, Chiggie rode the trolley out to the Alpine Hotel near the lagoon.

Chiggie summered in Oak Bluffs, first at the Alpine Hotel then camped on a small lot near the lagoon. After summers holding an umbrella and cooking in the rain, she had a small camp built, with a ladder to a window to crawl into her second-floor bedroom. She relished the rustic atmosphere of her summer abode. Having enjoyed her homemade cottage for three quarters of a century, Chiggie passed away at the age of 101, a Vineyarder by chance and then by choice.

Joan Boykin is obsessed with Martha's Vineyard. She first vacationed in Oak Bluffs as a child in the 1940s, and her memories are poignant decades later: "Mid-June every summer of my childhood, my mother and I would start our trip to the Vineyard for the entire summer. Our train travels would begin in Newark, New Jersey, and end in Woods Hole."

Her recollection of the trip is clear, boarding the "New York/New Haven & Hartford's train on the Old Colony line called the Day Cape Codder, which would take us all the way from New York City to Woods Hole, MA. That's right, all the way to Woods Hole." She is still amazed by the train service: "The trains had dining cars with each table dressed in fancy tablecloths and crisply ironed napkins. The waiters and conductors were always the same and seemed to remember me from year to year… made me feel special and grown up." Train service to Woods Hole ceased in 1964.

Joan adds, "The train stopped at what is now the staging area for cars waiting to get onto the ferries. It was literally only steps from train to boat. A comfortable and luxurious way to travel in the days when lots of people didn't have cars and the road system left a lot to be desired anyway."

Barbara Townes summered in the Highlands and swam at Highland Beach. She recalled, "You were never allowed to go anywhere in a bathing suit. At the beach you would pay ten cents for a locker and you dressed in the bath houses."

Not all of her memories were happy. "I remember when they told the people who used Highland Beach that they could not use it anymore. It had been a public beach, but now they were leasing it to a group of people from East Chop; they refused to have any black people on the beach." Those restrictions included Jewish people as well. The East Chop Association was formed in 1941.

Yet, when Barbara Townes was interviewed in 1983, she said, "This is the place to be, here. It's the place. And my mother who had been in every resort from Maine to Florida said, 'there was no place like Oak Bluffs.' And I believed her."[99]

Will Jones was a summer resident of Oak Bluffs, coming of age in the '40s and '50s. "Before World War II, Oak Bluffs was known as a tourist trap," he recalled. Servicemen from Otis Air Force Base on the Cape came over to Oak Bluffs for the day. They bowled on rainy days.

Jones's family owned the bowling alley where the Surfside Hotel is today. There was a sign out front, and "people came," said Jones. "Busy, especially in bad weather. Busier at night." Will Jones started as a pinsetter. "Lot of

Jones Bowling Alley was a fixture in downtown Oak Bluffs in the mid-twentieth century. Will Jones set pins as a child and manned the register as an adult. Courtesy of Will Jones.

local kids came in and set the pins for us. Buster and Rich Giordano were two of them." Later, Jones was responsible for cleaning the facility in the morning and eventually worked the cash register at night.

Across the street, the Tivoli was the center of activity, with a soda fountain and a lot happening. Dances at the Tivoli were a local highlight. Along with a number of shops, "there was a blind fellow who made little change purses, just by feel. They were pretty good."

Will Jones last visited the Vineyard in the 1970s, but his memories are both sharp and sweet.

After the conflagration of the Sea View House in 1892, a new hotel, bearing the same name, was constructed, facing the Inkwell and adjacent to Waban Park.

Johnny Perry, born in 1928, began his career as a tree surgeon. "I started climbing trees as a kid, pruning apple trees. I like it up in the air. It's aerodynamic." He first came to the Vineyard in 1953, "just before the big hurricane....I just came out here cold turkey. I tended bar at the old Sea View Hotel in Oak Bluffs from 1967 to 1984. Guys who came into the bar would call out 'Hey, Johnny.' So my name turned into Johnny Seaview, and it stuck."

The new Sea View House stood on Waban Park by the Inkwell. (Note the observation tower to the right.) Courtesy of the Martha's Vineyard Museum.

Perry worked for the owner, Loretta Balla, until she sold the hotel in the mid-1980s. He said, "I was a busy little bee tending that bar. There were bands in the summer almost six nights a week. All kinds of people came in— from actress Mia Farrow to Senator Edward Brooke. He had a party in the bar and rented it for the night. Loretta sold the Sea View in '84 or '85."[100]

When the hotel was demolished in the 1980s, it was replaced by condominiums, also named Sea View, and again adorned with a cupola similar to the previous Sea View Hotel.

EDWIN DEVRIES VANDERHOOP WAS the only Wampanoag elected to serve as state legislator. Following his single term in 1888, he built a house on the cliffs in the 1890s. A century later, his house was converted to the Aquinnah Cultural Center, an educational museum for tourists. The house was certified by the National Register of Historic Places in 2006.

Today in Aquinnah (formerly Gay Head) "the rhythm of visitors is governed by the arrival of tour buses, and in high season each bus drops off up to forty people at a time for a half-hour visit," wrote Richard Skidmore about summer activity at the Gay Head Cliffs.[101]

Skidmore enumerated shops that line the bricked walkway up to the refurbished observation point, where eager tourists take multiple images of the multicolored clay cliffs, the lighthouse and the ocean. It is the pride of the Vineyard—the must-see sight.

The Aquinnah Shop, run by the Vanderhoop family, opened in 1945. It serves food on a deck that overlooks the shoreline below—a most impressive dining establishment. Stony Creek Gifts opened in the 1950s. Sisters Berta Welch and Carla Cuch carry a variety of Native American merchandise with novel signs, wind chimes and a variety of jewelry.

Hat-Mar-Cha Gifts is run by Martha and Marshall Lee. It was opened in 1974 by Martha's parents. Her grandfather, Charles Vanderhoop, was the Gay Head lighthouse keeper. Martha says tourists who visit Gay Head are "surprised to find native people here on Martha's Vineyard in the most beautiful part of the Island. Part of working up here is being a bit of an educator, and I like that."

Adriana Ignatio chose not to compete with her sisters at Stony Creek Gifts; she opened On the Cliffs in 1990, offering a variety of women's fashions and accessories, sweatshirts and T-shirts.

Wayward Wampum, run by Jason Widdiss, offers handcrafted wampum jewelry for sale, as well as special orders. Jason continues the craft popularized by his father, Donald Widdiss.

The tribe has made a concerted effort to educate the public. The Aquinnah Cultural Center is just steps away from the shops, offering an extensive display of historical tribal items.

In 2013, a Native American kiosk was built at the cliffs, complete with bark shingles and a rounded roof, representative of a wetu, the original housing of the Wampanoag. Even with tribal members in all the shops, having a tribal presence on site is helpful. The kiosk offers cultural information and environmental efforts by the tribe as they continue to live in their native land.

Martha's Vineyard began to regain its stature as a resort community when the national press mentioned the prominent people and the relaxing atmosphere afforded Vineyard visitors. Two brief accounts describe aspects of the Vineyard lifestyle.

In the 1950s, local guidebooks and the chamber of commerce praised the Striped Bass and Bluefish Derby, with its "superb and varied fishing" and "one of the great original American fishing contests."

Cocktail parties predominated. "For no one on Martha's Vineyard—whether in years past or years present, or, for that matter, years to come,—could ever be anywhere else. This more than anything is an article of faith long held and no procession of martinis can ever, even slightly, erode this."[102]

The postwar tourist was an everyman of American society, neither rich nor poor, neither famous nor unknown. No single description characterized the visitors who sought the Vineyard between 1945 and 1970. The island retained its isolationist state, removed and apart from mainland America. It was off the grid, off the radar, yet those who visited the Vineyard treasured its unique atmosphere, quiet delights, scenic shores and uninhibited lifestyle and landscape.

Martha's Vineyard was a world apart. The two mailboxes in Oak Bluffs said it all: "Local" and "America and Beyond."

A Tale of Two Bridges (1969–75)

Not so large that the identity of a patron is lost.[103]
—Metropolitan Hotel advertisement

All that peace and tranquility, all that innocence and naivete, all that simplicity was dashed by two significant events that effectively put Martha's Vineyard on the map—both nationally and internationally. The first was a tragic accident in 1969, and the second was the filming of a major motion picture five years later.

A tale of two bridges describes the dramatic impact of Senator Ted Kennedy's auto accident off the Dike Bridge on Chappaquiddick and Steven Spielberg's filming of Jaws along the State Beach bridge in 1974. These two bridges brought fame and fortune to islanders and set the stage for the latter quarter of the twentieth century as the burgeoning tourist trade exploded. Virtually all of the hype and excitement of today's tourist market can be traced back to Chappaquiddick and the Jaws bridge, which is why these twin events are integral to the study of modern Vineyard tourism.

Ted Kennedy chose Chappaquiddick as a site to rendezvous with staffers from his brother's presidential campaign. When Robert Kennedy was assassinated in Los Angeles on June 5, 1968, the hopes and dreams of a second Kennedy presidency were dashed. Ted was devastated, yet he sought to bring together his brother's staffers to remember Bobby's campaign and, perhaps, to plant the seeds for his own presidential ambitions.

The Dike Bridge spans an inlet on Chappaquiddick. This was the scene of the tragedy that rocked the Kennedy mystique. Courtesy of Joyce Dresser.

The gathering took place on Chappaquiddick in mid-July, 1969. If Martha's Vineyard had a reputation for being remote, Chappy was that much more removed. The traveler had to take the steamship from Woods Hole to the Vineyard and then drive across the island to Edgartown. Down at the harbor the traveler would wait for the three-car ferry, the On Time, to cross Edgartown Harbor on a ninety-second junket. The site for Kennedy's meeting was near Dike Bridge, a couple of miles along the rustic roadway of Chappy.

Kennedy had booked a room at the Shiretown Inn in Edgartown and planned to spend the night there. Late in the evening of July 18, he offered to give Mary Jo Kopechne, one of the staffers, a ride. When he left the party, for whatever reason, he turned right, onto the road to Dike Bridge, away from the ferry slip. His car went off the bridge, which had no railing, and plunged into the waters of Poucha Pond. The car sank. Kennedy managed to crawl out; Mary Jo Kopechne did not. She drowned.

The incident on Chappaquiddick was the same weekend of the first moon landing, July 20, 1969, with "one small step for man, one giant step for mankind."

Senator Ted Kennedy was arrested for leaving the scene of the accident on Chappaquiddick in 1969. Courtesy of the Connie Sanborn collection.

Kennedy, at thirty-seven, was fit enough to walk the two miles back to the ferry slip, which was shut down for the evening. He swam across Edgartown Harbor and made his way to his hotel. In the morning, he called the police to report the accident. That's when the story broke—the submerged car was discovered, the woman's body recovered and Kennedy went into seclusion. Questions surfaced about his actions and a court inquisition was launched.

When Edgartown police chief Dominic Arena (1929–2019) passed away, his obituary carried a quote that the incident "changed my life.... [I'll] forever be connected with it." Chief Arena repeatedly dove into the water to search for Kopechne. And it was Chief Arena who arrested Senator Kennedy for leaving the scene of the accident. Arena considered the death "an accident, a true accident caused by natural conditions."[104]

Chief Arena said he would always be identified as "the Chappaquiddick chief." And he was.[105]

Months after the accident, there was a finding that Kennedy had acted inappropriately but not criminally. His presidential dreams evaporated, and Chappaquiddick became a buzz word for the fissure of the Kennedy mystique.

What the bridge at Chappaquiddick engendered was a dramatic rise in tourism. Curiosity about this remote island off the shores of Martha's Vineyard stimulated visitors and tourists from that day to this. Vineyarders were part of the story and are often eager to share their opinions and perspectives on the Kennedy tragedy. Locals became tour guides, self-proclaimed experts to myriad ambulance chasers, explorers and investigators—real and imagined. A new economic engine sprang to life.

Tourists, excursionists, vacationers and curiosity seekers want to see the bridge; many people appropriated pieces of the structure as morbid souvenirs. The bridge was rebuilt in the 1980s, with a guardrail, and today serves as the means of entry onto East Beach on Chappaquiddick.

All these curious people needed places to stay, food to eat, transportation and information about Martha's Vineyard. The tourist trade exploded, and in the course of a short time, the population of the Vineyard experienced a sharp increase. The business community stepped in to offer more opportunities for newcomers, and the island of Martha's Vineyard assumed a dramatic new role on the national stage. If nothing else, the tragedy on Dike Bridge put Martha's Vineyard on the national radar. Kennedy's accident proved a promotional boon to the Vineyard from the perspective of a growing economic blessing. To this day, it can be traced back to the crisis of July 18, 1969.

JAWS, WRITTEN BY PETER Benchley, who summered in Nantucket, tells the dramatic story of a shark that frightens the throngs of beachgoers along the Long Island shoreline over July 4. When it was decided to produce a major motion picture from the book in the early 1970s, the plan was to film on a remote island, building on the fear and isolation of a beachfront community besieged by a great white shark. The film crew initially set off for Nantucket; however, a looming fog bank precluded Steven Spielberg from visiting the "gray lady," and the filmmakers landed on the Vineyard instead. The rest is history.

"After 35 years, people haven't tired of talking about or watching Steven Spielberg's quintessential summer movie Jaws. The movie flooded theaters for the first time in June 1975, and the buzz around it remains particularly strong on the original Jaws movie set—the beaches and towns across Martha's Vineyard, which portrayed the fictional Amity Island in the 1975 film based on Peter Benchley's best-selling novel." Reuters reporter Lauren Keiper continued, "On the Vineyard, it's almost as easy find a resident who played an extra in the flick as it is to buy an ice-cream cone." She noted that many of the extras were local kids, who got to play in the water for five dollars a day and then segue into panic mode when they encountered the artificial shark approaching them.[106]

Jaws was filmed in the summer of 1974, mostly right on Martha's Vineyard. Edgartown was transformed into the fictional village of Amity. Movie stars included Roy Schneider, Richard Dreyfuss and Robert Shaw. The business of filming Jaws provided a solid source of revenue for struggling island businesses. Myriad mini crises and disasters erupted over the film schedule and budget, and at times, it was doubtful whether the twenty-seven-year-old Spielberg would finish his ambitious venture.

The iconic Jaws bridge lives on decades after the movie broke box office records in the summer of 1975. Officially known as the American Legion

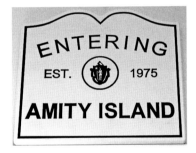

Right: Amity Island was the name of the fictional town in the movie Jaws. Souvenir in a shop; courtesy of Thomas Dresser.

Below: The State Beach bridge, colloquially known as Big Bridge, Second Bridge or Jaws bridge, was featured in the iconic movie. Courtesy of the Connie Sanborn Collection.

Memorial Bridge, Jaws bridge links Oak Bluffs and Edgartown along State Beach on the northeast shore of Martha's Vineyard. Designated as "Big Bridge" by locals, and "Second Bridge" by historians,[107] the experience of jumping off the bridge has become a rite of passage and draws crowds of beachgoers each sunny summer day. While no plaque or sign commemorates the Jaws bridge, and it has been remodeled and rebuilt, it is easily identified as the site where the Amity police chief's son was attacked by the shark. In the movie, Roy Schneider, the chief, is seen dashing across the bridge with an anxious look of distress on his face. The realistic images of that scene live on nearly a half century after it first frightened thousands of movie fans.

Martha's Vineyard was selected as the site for the film because it offered an atmosphere where the fear of the shark would prove detrimental to the business of tourism. That was the premise of the movie—keep the beaches open, especially over July 4 weekend. That role was well defined by Mayor Larry Vaughn (Murray Hamilton). Making the shark scenes scarier added to the excitement, while its fictional storyline actually boosted tourism.

In filming the shark and boat scenes, the movie producers appreciated the relatively shallow waters offshore—no more than thirty-five feet deep—which meant the mechanical shark scenes could be filmed with minimal problems, out of sight of land.

One of Spielberg's goals was to create an atmosphere in which the shark appeared to be close to where people were swimming, which intensified the fear factor. At times, Spielberg only hinted at the presence of the shark, which magnified the sense of danger. John Williams's musical score evoked a sense of danger. Neither wardrobe nor scenery used the color red, which added to the shock when the shark succeeding in its bloody mission.

Three shark models were designed and developed that could move pneumatically. One was the full-size shark towed through the water; the other two were right- or left-facing, depending on camera angle. When the shark models reached the Vineyard from California, the platform that supported them tipped over, dousing them and causing an immediate delay to hoist them out of the water. The pneumatic hoses absorbed saltwater, which the design crew had not anticipated. Did they not know that Martha's Vineyard was in the Atlantic Ocean, with salt in it? The crew developed a kinship with the model shark, nicknamed Bruce for Bruce Ramer, Spielberg's attorney.

The cost of special effects ballooned to more than $3 million due to innumerable issues with the mechanical sharks. And those sharks were so ornery some movie crew took to calling the project "Flaws." As the film wrapped, it was considered a Hitchcock-like thriller rather than an amateur over-budget fiasco.

And the movie was over budget. Instead of costing $3.5 million, it cost $9 million. Jaws was scheduled to wrap before the summer season got underway, but the final scene was not shot until October 6, 1974—159 days after Spielberg commenced shooting, which was three times the scheduled time frame. On that last day, Spielberg chose to not attend the dramatic conclusion because he feared the movie crew planned to toss him into the ocean after the scene was shot. (Superstitiously, Spielberg has failed to show on the last shoot of all of his subsequent movies.)

One of the more iconic lines from Jaws is Chief Brody's, "You're gonna need a bigger boat," improvised by Roy Schneider as the shark leapt at the Orca; it was not in the original script. Because the line was not sufficiently audible during initial audience viewing, the volume of the line was raised.

Another improvement was made after the movie wrapped. Matt Hooper (Richard Dreyfuss) was a marine biologist brought in to assess the danger posed by the shark. When Hooper was underwater and approached a boat with a damaged hull, Spielberg reshot the scene to include Ben Gardner with a latex model of Vineyarder Craig Kingsbury's head that rolled out to confront Dreyfuss. That memorable scene elicits screams to this day. Actor Robert Shaw, as the salty Quint, modeled his naughty nautical lingo on Kingsbury. Incidentally, this additional scene was shot in a swimming pool in California. To re-create the murky Vineyard waters, powered milk was sprinkled into the pool.

THE NATIONAL OCEANIC AND Atmospheric Administration studies the shark population along the East Coast of the United States. Before 2004, shark sightings numbered one or two a year; recently, the average has jumped to twenty sightings per year. The increase in the shark population is attributed to improved conservation efforts and an increase in the seal population, a ready element of the shark diet.[108]

In 2018, two shark attacks occurred off Cape Cod—one causing serious internal injuries to a man on a boogie board off Truro, who fought off the shark, and the second causing the death of Andrew Medici a twenty-six-year-old engineering student, again on a boogie board, off Wellfleet. Medici's death was the first fatal shark attack off Massachusetts waters since 1936. And while shark attacks are rare, the creature poses a serious threat to swimmers, and the presence of sharks in the water must be addressed with care and caution.

Increased shark sightings and the continued popularity of Jaws has proven to be a big boost for tourism. The connection to Martha's Vineyard is undeniable. Businesses on the Cape and islands encourage this with paraphernalia, festivals and tours that keep the theme of the movie alive. It doesn't hurt that Martha's Vineyard is a remote island with a dependence on tourism, which is the punch line of the movie itself. That's why the beaches were not closed over July 4 weekend, even though a woman was attacked by a shark in the movie.

Since the release of Jaws, tourists have flocked to the Vineyard to visit scenes from the film. Annual screenings and tours of local sites in the iconic movie are part of the fanfare that continues to draw tourists to Martha's Vineyard, as seen in a January 2, 2018 letter to the editor of the Martha's Vineyard Times:

> I would just like to thank Martha's Vineyard for being the filming location in the 1975 classic film Jaws. I cannot tell you how many times I have watched that movie, and felt a sense of fear that only Steven Spielberg can provide. Yes, the shark was terrifying, but Martha's Vineyard is now even more iconic. I love your beautiful area, and I can only say that if Jaws had been filmed in a busy port, or a different town, it would have been much different. It must be very cool to have your area associated with such a film with an enduring legacy. You have certainly had an impact on many lives, and certainly mine.
>
> Samuel Ludke, Wisconsin Rapids, Wisconsin

The tourist in 2020 is still curious about the incident on Chappaquiddick. "Where is the bridge?" is a common query. And many people who come to the Vineyard for the first time know about the movie Jaws and want to see where it was filmed along State Beach by Big Bridge. They have heard the tales, and now they want to see the specific sights. Incidents on two bridges—one frighteningly real the other fabulously fictitious—lead to two disparate inquiries by tourists flocking to Martha's Vineyard.

Presidential Vacations (1990–2020)

Roofspopupwhereonlytreesgrewnotlongago. Buttheislandstillisn'truined.
In the words of a dour New Englander, "not yet."[109]
—Shirley Ann Grace

Just as tourists are intrigued by the horror and drama of the Chappaquiddick incident and the summer blockbuster Jaws, so are they drawn to the Vineyard because of the presidential presence on the island.

When President Ulysses S. Grant visited the Vineyard on August 26, 1874, he had no way of knowing how much his visit, both in the short and long term, would influence the tourist community. His immediate goal was to enlist the Methodist community to support his intent to run for a third term in office, as his wife wished. There was not a lot of encouragement, so he dropped that idea.

According to local lore, President Grant enlisted his former bugler and dispatch rider, Frances Vincent Pease, an islander, to organize a band to play for the president when he visited the Vineyard. The Vineyard Haven Band had formed only a few years before, and according to Tom Bardwell, Pease's great-grandson, the band performed for Grant. Still performing today, band concerts are an enduring charm that entertain locals and tourists alike.[110]

Grant's decision to visit the Vineyard influenced thousands of people to consider that the Vineyard might be a good place to visit. They began to make the trek after Grant's visit. A century later, it was President Bill Clinton who chose the Vineyard as the site of his annual vacation and made presidential vacations a memorable occasion for people of all ages, as well as the media.

Vineyard visits by United States presidents have actually been quite numerous over the years, although the focus has been primarily on their time while in office. Most significant were those of Presidents Grant, Clinton and Obama.

John Adams is rumored to have traveled to Chilmark in 1760 to hobnob with his college roommate Jonathan Allen. Adams had not yet been elected president, nor had the United States even been created, but Adams recognized the import of visiting Martha's Vineyard.

Grant spent three days in Oak Bluffs in August 1874, venturing off-island to Naushon, Nantucket and Cape Cod, but celebrating his official visit with a grand affair at the Sea View Hotel in downtown Cottage City.

President Chester Alan Arthur was fishing off Menemsha Bight on the United States Fishing Commissioner's Fishhawk on September 6, 1882. He witnessed a federal agency conducting research on the declining population of herring, mackerel and striped bass. Arthur was familiar with the area, as he spent a week at the Cuttyhunk Fishing Club.

Calvin Coolidge was among the most frequent presidential visitors, although never while in office. As lieutenant governor of Massachusetts, Coolidge attended festivities on Martha's Vineyard at the tabernacle during Illumination Night and in 1918, as lieutenant governor, when Governor McCall awarded Gay Head a plaque for garnering 10 percent of the male population as World War I enlistees. Returning in 1929, out of office, Coolidge spent time in Lambert's Cove.

President Franklin Delano Roosevelt had two experiences in Vineyard waters but never on land. In June 1933, a squall forced his sailboat into Katama Bay. FDR was known to be a very capable sailor, but the storm was too much for his small boat. And on August 3, 1941, the president boarded the Augusta and steamed from Menemsha Bight to Newfoundland to meet British prime minister Winston Churchill to sign the Atlantic Charter, which established guidelines for the allies in World War II. (Meanwhile, FDR's Potomac motored through the Cape Cod Canal with a decoy president ostensibly on board, still fishing.)

Eleanor Roosevelt visited the Vineyard a number of times and commented on Nantucket. She noted, "The rivalry between these two islands seems fairly vigorous, so I will only say that I found both of them delightful." (Granddaughter Laura Roosevelt moved to the Vineyard in 1995.)

John F. Kennedy was in a small sailboat blown ashore in July 1941 and spent a night at the Ocean View Hotel under the auspices of Joseph Sylvia. Vineyard Haven tailor Samuel Issokson repaired the sailor's sail. Many other JFK visits occurred over the years: Jackie water-skied off Chappy in '61, William Styron enjoyed a picnic aboard ship with JFK in '62 and JFK sailed off Chappy in '63.

Jackie Kennedy bought over three hundred acres of land in Gay Head in the late 1970s and was a regular summer visitor, mingling with tourists at Gay Head and attending art exhibits and openings. She died in 1994, and the property is now enjoyed by her daughter, Caroline, and her family.

Son John F. Kennedy Jr. died in plane crash off Gay Head on July 16, 1999.

"Former President Richard M. Nixon was a traffic stopper on lower Main Street in Edgartown Saturday morning," wrote reviewer Phyllis Meras in the Vineyard Gazette. It was a big deal to see the former president slowly make his way up lower Main Street, chatting briefly with Joe Sollitto, clerk of superior court, and window-shopping along the way. A crowd gathered. "He was stopped by between eighty and a hundred admirers, autograph-seekers, picture takers, and those who were just curious. Outside The Kafe [now, the Wharf Pub and Restaurant], he paused for photographs and more conversation, mainly with island visitors."

Many passersby were unimpressed or worried that his presence was a sign of impending congestion of traffic and people. And, as this was 1980, that fear bore fruit in the next generation.[111]

Lady Bird Johnson, widow of President Lyndon Baines Johnson, was known for her devotion to wildlife and the environment. As first lady, her primary accomplishment was beautifying the national landscape. She promoted planting wildflowers along national roadways to improve the scenery and reduce the blight of billboards.

Her week-long Vineyard visits were peaceful and carefree during the day, yet she engaged in a vibrant social schedule later in the day, on occasion taking in two or three cocktail or dinner parties. Lady Bird made the most of her time on the Vineyard, appreciating the beauty of swans in their aquatic habitat and sailboats gracing the harbor shores.

As an advocate of the natural beauty of Martha's Vineyard, Lady Bird visited the island for thirty years, until 2007, the year she died.

"'THE CLINTONS ARE COMING!' The rumor of early summer 1993 must have been true, because every Vineyarder down to the last pinkletink was within two degrees of separation from someone who really, really knew." Once again worried, Vineyarders feared the crowds, the publicity and the loss of privacy. And yet, it was a sitting president of the United States who deigned to vacation on the Vineyard. That had to count for something.

"Throngs of giddy Vineyarders lined Airport Road to gawk, cheer, and wave signs as the Clinton motorcade headed from the terminal to the first family's vacation digs."

Bill and Hillary Clinton made themselves available to the rich and famous, as well as the man and woman on the street. They curried favor with author Bill Styron and singer Carly Simon, yet devoured ice cream at Mad Martha's and created a stir as they toured the displays and rides at the Agricultural Fair. They made the most of their vacation, for themselves and for the island.

The year after Clinton was impeached, their time on the Vineyard proved more reclusive. There was a sign of support nailed to a tree in Vineyard Haven by Craig Kingsbury of Jaws fame. The sign was in place for over a decade. It read, "Hoo Rah for Bill —Craig."

Former president Bill Clinton continues to vacation on the Vineyard. Derek and George Gamble met him at Farm Neck in 2017. Courtesy of George Gamble.

"During the presidential years, the so-called Summer White House ignited worldwide curiosity about the island, swelling tourism, the seasonal population, and in turn our overall economy," Shelley Christiansen wrote.[112]

Often, President Bill Clinton walked outside the line of Secret Service protection; he was always a people person. Clinton brought Hollywood and money to the island. One day in the summer of 2006, Bill Clinton walked by the chamber of commerce window, licking an ice cream cone, unaccompanied by the Secret Service. He pushed the envelope in a positive way.

Months after he declared for the presidency in 2007, trailing in the early polls, Barack Obama visited the Vineyard. He used his island vacation for a routine of golf and family time, as well as daily workouts and dining out. Obama mingled with the man on the street to some degree but preferred to relax with friends in private. He was comfortable in a safe environment. Obama enjoyed this downtime, which prepared him for his initial weeks as president, as he was immediately consumed by the financial collapse of the economy and subsequent recession.

A decade after Clinton left office, President Barack Obama selected Martha's Vineyard as his annual vacation site. He devoted hours to playing golf on Vineyard links and captivated the press with his subtle restaurant selections. Having the president opt for a Vineyard vacation, even one interrupted by the funeral for Senator Kennedy, made for a memorable experience. "That was a tremendous stimulus for Vineyard businesses that Obama gave us," says Nancy Gardella, director of the Vineyard Chamber of Commerce.

She warmed to her memory, "Two great things happened in 2008: the Global Recession and the Obamas came to the Vineyard. Once Obama decided to come here, that brought everyone else. He gave us a great lift. Everyone came to the Vineyard because of the young Obamas and their two cute daughters."

The recession caused a number of businesses to face serious financial challenges. Over one hundred chamber businesses failed in 2008 and 2009. These closures forced a realization on the Vineyard that a unified chamber was essential for a strong business climate to rebound from the recession.

The director recognizes the role Obama played in putting the Vineyard on the wide screen: "Everyone in the world was talking about Martha's Vineyard." And President Obama generated an apolitical response:

Even before he was a senator, in August 2004, Barack Obama visited the Vineyard. He signed a copy of his book at the Old Whaling Church for Shelley Christiansen. Courtesy of Shelley Christiansen.

"It doesn't matter who you voted for, having the president choose to vacation on the Vineyard is all that counts." A great many African Americans visited the Vineyard for the first time, following in the president's footsteps, hoping for a sighting or a rumor of his whereabouts. Tourist exposure was sought and afforded. President Obama spread the wealth. Businesses benefited. The Vineyard benefitted.

On his first presidential vacation in 2009, President Obama did not go to the Bunch of Grapes bookstore. Owner Dawn Branch wrote him a letter, requesting support of small businesses. The next year, President Obama showed up with his daughters and their book lists; together they picked out their summer reading. He paid cash. Dawn said his daughters were so polite and cute. Barack said it was all due to Michelle. "That made Dawn love him all the more!" says Ms. Gardella. Barack and Michelle Obama presented a wholesome family bolstered by a compatible, equitable marriage.

In 2009, THERE WERE few GPSs and iPhones. Reporters created a buzz about the Vineyard with the excitement of covering the Obamas. One Oak Bluffs restaurant, Nancy's Take-Out, became known across the country for the fries and clams the president ordered. A Milan, Italy newspaper published photographs of the Obamas cycling through the state forest. The only sour note was that the president was spotted riding without his helmet. The year before, in 2008, while still a senator, Obama stopped on the bike path to fix the flat tire of a stranded rider to help a fellow citizen.

The Presidential Press Corps held forth at the Oak Bluffs School, looking for any information beyond where the Obamas would go for golf and dinner. Nancy Gardella and the chamber provisioned an information office at the school gym for the press corps to learn about the Vineyard.

Besides golf, President Obama enjoyed dining at various Vineyard restaurants. Here he leaves Sweet Life in Oak Bluffs. The Obamas purchased property on the Vineyard in 2019. Courtesy of Leon Hawksley.

The chamber supplied books and maps and offered information on Vineyard businesses. In turn, businesses donated brownies and fudge to the press corps, which proved popular.

The chamber provided relevant information to the press corps whenever they needed details or descriptions. Reporters sought all kinds of information, and the chamber was happy to talk about Martha's Vineyard. The press corps was stationed at the Mansion House in 2011, and Assistant Press Secretary Josh Earnest needed a flag. The chamber had one. The chamber promoted business aspects that were publicized. The Farm Institute made sandwich boards with kids' messages painted on them; the boards were placed around the Vineyard and garnered a lot of attention. Sharkey's Mexican Cantina advertised unique concoctions: Barack Tacos and Obamamargarita.

Presidential vacations proved an economic stimulus for Martha's Vineyard that lasted well into the fall and beyond.

Over his two terms, President Obama continued to vacation on the Vineyard each year, with the exception of 2012, when, like President Clinton, he used vacation time to campaign. His vacations were low-key and family focused, with daily games of golf and evenings spent dining at one of many fine restaurants across the island. Not one to socialize with tourists or locals, the presence of the president on island brought a sense of auspicious excitement to Martha's Vineyard.

Subsequent to his time in the White House, Barack Obama has returned to the island each August, intent on playing golf and dining out. His broad smile mirrors the eager enthusiasm the public feels for him.

Tourists naturally followed both Presidents Clinton and Obama, and the Vineyard has become more popular and busier than ever before.

WHEN HE LEARNED OF a book on Vineyard tourism, local contractor Dave Dutton asked rhetorically, "What occupations make the Vineyard tick? Construction and Tourism, that's all there is."[113] Construction centers on those tourists who decide to build a second home or to upgrade the home they have.

The ultimate tourist experience, though, is to be married on Martha's Vineyard. The island has become a popular site for destination weddings. "The island sells itself as a wedding venue. With some of the most talented vendors in the industry, it grants an unforgettable experience that portrays the Vineyard in a positive light while stimulating the economy at the same time." Business and pleasure go hand in hand.[114]

Planning a wedding on Martha's Vineyard brings the tourist to the heart of the Vineyard economy. Years ago, weddings were a summer activity—small scale and local. Over the years, with the prominence of presidents and a certain movie, Martha's Vineyard has gained popularity as a premier wedding site. Tourists are impressed by the preponderance of weddings, especially in the shoulder season of September and early October. Business is booming.

Photographer Randi Baird asks rhetorically, "Where else can you find beautiful beaches, classic New England architecture, and breathtaking remote locations to add to the charm and allure of your special day? The island makes a perfect backdrop for the most formal to the most casual of weddings."

She continues, "The benefits of hiring a wedding planner on Martha's Vineyard are even greater than they might be off-island, quite simply because they get it. Our island can be hard to navigate—geographically, politically, and socially." Simply traveling to the Vineyard can be a challenge, hence, "you better believe what happens here does too." Wedding planners are familiar with the challenges of planning a destination wedding, especially in an island community.[115]

The Vineyard has much to offer as a wedding site. "The island's stunning views, diverse towns, outstanding restaurants and night life is enough to make the Vineyard a desirable wedding destination." The majority of weddings are held by "couples that have substantial ties to the island. Whether they have a family home, have spent summers growing up on the island, or have family history, those with no connection to the island often don't consider the Vineyard for a wedding." Nevertheless, Kim Scott of KG Events notes, "The volume of weddings produced on the island is extremely large, and is a booming industry on the island."

"The Vineyard has been rumored to be the second largest wedding destination next to Vegas," reports Ms. Scott. However, she adds, "I have done weddings in Charleston, SC, as well, and I heard the same rumors there."[116]

"Vineyard weddings are often accompanied by activities," observes Kim. Bridal couples consider that "if they are asking for their guests to travel all the way to the Vineyard for their wedding, they want to make the experience fun and worthwhile. It's an opportunity for the couple to 'show off' the island to their closest friends and family." Wedding planners coordinate activities such as golf outings, 5K runs, beach parties, sails, tours, hikes, fishing charters, clambakes, brunches, luncheons, rehearsal dinners and more. All of these are popular with tourists and serve to enlist wedding guests in the euphoria of tourism.

The busiest month for weddings is September, which unfortunately, can be chancy, adds Ms. Scott. "Bad weather has come out of nowhere, leaving us with little to no time to execute a Plan B or to fix a problem. Hurricane season also coincides with the most popular time to get married on the island, so it can be extremely challenging."

The Vineyard is a special place for a tourist, and an extra special site for a couple getting married. Isolated from the mainland and a quintessential New England experience with varied topography, the Vineyard offers "the historic and classic town of Edgartown, the vast green fields of Chilmark, the rock formations and cliffs of Aquinnah, the isolation of Chappy, and the pristine beaches," all of which, says Ms. Scott, "make the Vineyard so utopic—there is truly nowhere else like it." An outstanding aspect is the Vineyard culture, "laid back, but hard working, and never taking for granted the beauty of the island we call home."

For the wedding planner, "There's no greater feeling on an event day than seeing your clients celebrating the biggest day of their life surrounded by their favorite people on such a special island." Bridal couples are also a great promotional aspect for the Vineyard. Weddings support Vineyard businesses. Their presence on the island, with their guests, encourages return visits, further tours and the enjoyment fostered by a delightful resort community.

When is it all too much for the island to bear? How many tourists can the Vineyard handle? Development is restricted, and 40 percent of the island land mass is under conservation restriction. Yet with a daily summer population of more than one hundred thousand visitors, the numbers almost suggest a limit or restriction on tourists may be in order.

The Steamship Authority, which operates the daily ferry service, monitors the traffic situation through auto and truck reservations and passenger traffic. Vehicle traffic is astounding. In July and August, more than fifty thousand cars ride the steamship each month, well over one thousand a day. Annual

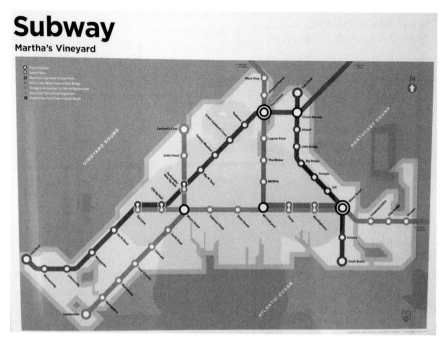

Whether to confuse or amuse, an artist created a subway map of the Vineyard. Souvenir decals for a nude beach and the tunnel are also popular. Art created by Transit Authority Figures, photograph by Thomas Dresser.

Island Transport's sightseeing buses are a familiar sight on Vineyard roadways. Courtesy of Thomas Dresser.

auto traffic is more than four hundred thousand vehicles. And trucks, carting supplies across the sound to feed and provision all the visitors, number more than 10,000 per month, or 130,000 per year. Vineyard sidewalks bulge with tourists, who seek to savor the tranquility of the island oasis. Leviathan tour buses rumble along narrow Vineyard roadways, to the consternation of locals. Should tourist traffic be curtailed?

OF COURSE, THE EMERGENCE of COVID-19 in the spring of 2020 will have an unknown impact on tourism on Martha's Vineyard. The combined issues of social distancing and economic chaos are sure to linger. Islanders need time and money to prepare for the onslaught of summer. Tourists need assurance of a healthy environment and financial well-being before they plan to vacation or visit the Vineyard. The new normal may be very different from the recent past. It is that uncertainty that complicates a tourist's plans going forward. Both tourist and vendor have to adopt a wait-and-see attitude to the future.

Another angle to consider is how the local population reacts to tourism. While Nancy Gardella of the chamber of commerce notes that everyone on the island is within two degrees of separation from the tourist industry, not everyone is pleased with that status report. A workshop titled "Balancing Quality of Life and Tourism" is offered in Bar Harbor, Maine, a tourist mecca like the Vineyard, which is also an island summer resort community with a mid-nineteenth-century heritage. "The purpose of the workshop is to learn and practice healthy public discussion and to understand the balance residents seek between continued engagement with tourism as part of the economy, and quality of life for those who live and work here." It's a concept whose time may have come.[117]

From the Wampanoag to Daniel Webster's visit in 1849, from the Methodist Campground to the Oak Bluffs Land & Wharf Company, from presidential visits to wedding planners, Martha's Vineyard has been and continues to be a resort community tourists visit to see and be seen, to experience and enjoy, to revel and remember.

EPILOGUE

Eighty-five years ago, Henry Beetle Hough wrote, "The basic attractions of Martha's Vineyard as a summer resort have remained, oddly enough, exactly what they were a hundred years ago." And most of the same sights in 1935 are on today's tourist's agenda in 2020: "Gay Head Cliffs and the Gay Head light, the Indian town, the surf on the South Beach, blue fishing the land and the water, the sky, the hills and the plain." (The Indian town became the federally recognized Wampanoag Tribe of Gay Head/ Aquinnah in 1987. Located in Aquinnah on Black Brook Road, the tribal headquarters hold tribal housing, a library and headquarters for the tribe.)[118]

Why do tourists continue to visit Martha's Vineyard? The island is a mere forty-five-minute ferry ride from Cape Cod and "is known for its low-key, private style and remains a sought-after vacation destination. Scenic beaches, spectacular sunsets and vacationing U.S. presidents have long been a feature, but Jaws has contributed steadily over the years to an economy reliant on tourism dollars."[119]

The Vineyard Gazette publishes an annual tourist guide to introduce visitors to Martha's Vineyard. The Martha's Vineyard Times offers the Vineyard Visitor, filled with current events and activities for the tourist. Both publications include maps and tours to help the novice get around, including a list of the five Vineyard lighthouses and various activities as part of the Vineyard scene. A common concern is restaurants, and both guides lists dining options.

IN THIS BOOK WE emphasize the historic relevance of tourism. A recent study surveyed the personal benefits to tourists, vacationers and excursionists and found that travel "improves both physical and mental health." The study reveals that "vacationing helps lower blood pressure and depression and stress levels." People who travel often are happier than less-frequent travelers. Workers return from their trips more creative, focused and dedicated to the work at hand rather than lounging around home. Not everyone has come to recognize and acknowledge the link between travel and better health. Freeing people from taxing anxiety improves their mental acumen to better adapt to a new environment. Physical movement is an attribute of the avid tourist. Those who don't travel face limitations from a stagnant lifestyle, mentally and physically. These results promote tourism—and the Vineyard is high on the list of places to see.[120]

NOTES

Chapter 1

1. Pocket Directory Guide, 9.
2. Foster, Meeting of Land and Sea, 88.
3. For an intriguing piece on Vineyard settlers before the Mayhews, see A.C. Trapp, "The First English Settlers of Martha's Vineyard: The Case for the Pease Tradition," Martha's Vineyard Quarterly, November 2018.
4. Van Riper, Edgartown, 8.
5. Foster, Meeting of Land and Sea, 156.
6. Vineyard Gazette, October 7, 1847.
7. Foster, Meeting of Land and Sea, 166.

Chapter 2

8. Guide of Cottage City, 9.
9. Stoddard, Centennial History, 27.
10. Brown, "Tourist's New England," 106.
11. Massachusetts Historical Commission, "MHC Reconnaissance."
12. Hough, Martha's Vineyard, 12.
13. Massachusetts Historical Commission, "MHC Reconnaissance."
14. Vineyard Gazette, April 26, 1935.
15. Brown, "Tourist's New England," 101.
16. Vineyard Gazette, April 26, 1935.

Chapter 3

17. The Vineyard as It Was, Is, and Is to Be, 3.
18. Vineyard Gazette, May 22, 1931.
19. Railton, History of Martha's Vineyard, 177.
20. Meras, "The Allure of the Azores," Martha's Vineyard Magazine, September 1, 2012.
21. Christopher Muther, "The Azores are Lush, Lovely and Ready to be Discovered," Boston Globe, March 24, 2019.
22. Meras, "Allure of the Azores."

Chapter 4

23. Tourist Guide of Cottage City.
24. Railton, History of Martha's Vineyard, 242.
25. Skip Finley, "Captains of Cottage City," Martha's Vineyard Quarterly, August 2018.
26. Brown, "Tourist's New England," 123.
27. Finley, "Captains of Cottage City," 20.
28. Brown, "Tourist's New England," 119.
29. Finley, "Captains of Cottage City," 12.
30. Brown, "Tourist's New England," 124.
31. Jones, Oak Bluffs, 89.
32. Brown, "Tourist's New England," 131.
33. Ibid., 127.
34. Railton, History of Martha's Vineyard, 248.

Chapter 5

35. Martha's Vineyard: Isle of Dreams and Health.
36. Tom Dunlop, "A Flagpole Tribute on West Chop," Martha's Vineyard Magazine, August 1, 2011.
37. Hough, Martha's Vineyard, 248.
38. Gale Huntington, "Up-Island Summer People," Dukes County Intelligencer, February 1980.
39. Hough, Martha's Vineyard, 239.
40. Ibid., 166.

Chapter 6

41. Tours and Guide to Southern Massachusetts, 23.
42. Hough, Martha's Vineyard, 52.
43. Tours and Guide to Southern Massachusetts, 27.
44. Gene Baer, "Old Island Trolley," Dukes County Intelligencer, May 1977.
45. Vineyard Gazette, September 28, 2018, reprinted from Vineyard Gazette, September 29, 1892.
46. Island Review.
47. Dukes County Intelligencer, August 1993.
48. Chris Baer, "This Was Then: Whaleboat Races," Martha's Vineyard Times, October 18, 2018.
49. Martha's Vineyard Times, September 27, 2018.
50. Hough, Martha's Vineyard, 205.
51. Nelson Bishop, "Roller Skating on Martha's Vineyard," Dukes County Intelligencer, August 1961.
52. Macy, Captains Daughters of Martha's Vineyard, 73.
53. Ibid., 74.
54. Francis Endicott, "Oh Man, You Should Have Been Here Yesteryear," Martha's Vineyard Magazine.
55. Kib Bramhall, "The Old Squibnocket Club," Martha's Vineyard Magazine.
56. Hough, Martha's Vineyard, 260.
57. Ibid., 126.

Chapter 7

58. Illustrated Travel Guide.
59. Vineyard Gazette, July 6, 1937.
60. Hough, Martha's Vineyard, 267.
61. Ibid., 272.

Chapter 8

62. Ibid., 204.
63. Ibid., 251.
64. Dresser, Music on Martha's Vineyard, 28.
65. Boykin, mvobsession.com, May 13, 2008.

66. Wysocki, "Oak Bluffs Reliving the Dream."

67. Dukes County Intelligencer, November 1994.

68. Hough, Martha's Vineyard, 200.

69. Sigelman, Martha's Vineyard Outdoors, 192–4.

70. Ibid., 196.

71. Van Riper, Edgartown, 82.

72. Ibid.

73. Chris Baer, "This Was Then: Girdlestone Park," Martha's Vineyard Times, May 28, 2014.

74. Chris Baer, "This Was Then: Baseball," Martha's Vineyard Times, August 23, 2018.

75. Jim Hickey, "From Ice Fields to Integration, Islanders Love the Call 'Play Ball!'" Vineyard Gazette, April 16, 2009.

76. Clyde L. MacKenzie Jr., "Island Basketball," Dukes County Intelligencer, February 1999.

77. Boston Globe, June 19, 1924.

Chapter 9

78. New York Martha's Vineyard Island Via New Haven Railroad.

79. Cromwell, "The History of Oak Bluffs as a Popular Resort for Blacks," Dukes County Intelligencer, August 1984.

80. Ibid., 3.

81. Morgan, "Continuing the Tradition."

82. Cromwell, "History of Oak Bluffs," 14–16.

83. Sam Bungey, "An Island too Small to be Segregated," Vineyard Gazette, August 20, 2009.

84. Ibid.

85. Dorothy West, "Cottagers Corner," Vineyard Gazette, June 25, 1971.

86. Skip Finley, "Oak Bluffs Town Column," Vineyard Gazette, February 19, 2014.

87. Troy McMullen, "Historically Black Beach Enclaves Are Fighting to Save Their History and Identity," Boston Globe, August 22, 2017.

88. Ibid.

89. Historic New England, "African American Vacationers,"

90. McMullen, "Historically Black Beach."

91. Ibid.

92. New England Historical Society, "The Green Book Guides."

93. Ebony, 1947.

94. Cromwell, "History of Oak Bluffs," 20.

95. Jackie Calmes, "Revisiting Black History on Martha's Vineyard," New York Times, August 29, 2010.

96. Cromwell, "History of Oak Bluffs," 22.

97. Ibid., 25.

Chapter 10

98. Martha's Vineyard Chamber of Commerce Guide.

99. Lee, More Vineyard Voices, 148, 150.

100. Brooks Robards, "How I Got Here: Johnny 'Seaview' Perry," Martha's Vineyard Magazine.

101. Richard Skidmore, "Cultural Outpost," Martha's Vineyard Magazine, July 1, 2013.

102. Town & Country, August, 1971.

Chapter 11

103. Metropolitan Hotel advertisement.

104. "Dominick J. Arena, Police Chief Who Arrested Ted Kennedy After Chappaquiddick, Dies at 89," Boston Globe, March 14, 2019.

105. Ibid.

106. Keiper, "'Jaws' Still Churns Waters."

107. Mayhew, Martha's Vineyard: A Short History and Guide, 109, Jaws Bridge is the second bridge you reach as you drive from Oak Bluffs to Edgartown. It's also known as "Three-Mile Bridge," as it is three miles from downtown Oak Bluffs.

108. Streep, "Great White Shark."

Chapter 12

109. Shirley Ann Grace, New York Times Magazine, August 15, 1965.

110. Christiansen, "Welcome, Mr. President!!!" Martha's Vineyard Magazine, August 1, 2009.

111. Ibid.

112. Ibid.
113. Author conversation with David Dutton in the Oak Bluffs Post Office, November 10, 2018.
114. Author interview with Kimberly Scott of KGEvents and Design, January 30, 2019.
115. Baird, "Planning a Martha's Vineyard Wedding."
116. We checked the number of marriage intentions in three areas. Las Vegas had 73,083 marriage intentions filed in 2018. Charleston County, South Carolina, recorded 4,871 marriage intentions in 2018. And then there's Martha's Vineyard. To calculate the number of marriage intentions filed by town, we contacted the town clerks who shared figures for 2018: Aquinnah (5), West Tisbury (17), Chilmark (19), Tisbury (53), Oak Bluffs (76) and Edgartown (117). The total marriage intentions on the Vineyard for 2018 was 287. That number is impressive but does not count weddings that originated in off-island Massachusetts towns. Clark County Nevada, "Raw Data Files for Statistical Analysis 2007–2019," County Clerk, http://www.clarkcountynv.gov/clerk/Pages/licensestatistics.aspx; Regina LeBlance is the Charleston County clerk.
117. National Institute for Civil Discourse; "How to Balance Tourism with Quality of Life," Bar Harbor Times, September 27, 2018.

Epilogue

118. Hough, Martha's Vineyard, 272.
119. Keiper, "'Jaws' Still Churns Waters."
120. Boston Sunday Globe, January 27, 2019.

Bibliography

Books

Dresser, Thomas. *Music on Martha's Vineyard.* Charleston, SC: The History Press, 2014.

———. *Travel History of Martha's Vineyard.* Charleston, SC: The History Press, 2019.

———. *Women of Martha's Vineyard.* Charleston, SC: The History Press, 2013.

Ewen, William. *Steamboats to Martha's Vineyard and Nantucket.* Charleston, SC: Arcadia Publishing, 2015.

Foster, David. *A Meeting of Land and Sea.* New Haven, CT: Yale University Press, 2017.

Hough, Henry Beetle. *Martha's Vineyard: Summer Resort (1835–1935).* Rutland, VT: Academy Books, 1936.

Jones, Peter. *Oak Bluffs: The Cottage City Years.* Charleston, SC: Arcadia Publishing, 2007.

Lee, Linsey. *More Vineyard Voices.* Edgartown, MA: Martha's Vineyard Historical Society, 2005.

Macy, Eliot Eldridge. *The Captain's Daughters of Martha's Vineyard.* Greenwich, CT: Chatham Press, 1978.

Mayhew, Eleanor Ransom. *Martha's Vineyard: A Short History and Guide.* Edgartown, MA: Dukes County Historical Society, 1956.

Railton, Arthur. *The History of Martha's Vineyard.* Beverly, MA: Commonwealth Editions (in association with the Martha's Vineyard Historical Society), 2006.

Sigelman, Nelson. Martha's Vineyard Outdoors. Vineyard Haven, MA: Tashmoo Publishing, 2017.

Stoddard, Chris. Centennial History of Cottage City. Oak Bluffs, MA: MV Printing, 1980.

Van Riper, Bow. Edgartown. Charleston, SC: Arcadia Publishing, 2018.

Online Sources

Baird, Randi. "Planning a Martha's Vineyard Wedding? There's a Coordinator for That." Randi Baird Photography (blog), February 2, 2019. https://randibaird.com.

Brown, Dona. "The Tourist's New England: Creating an Industry, 1820–1900." PhD diss., University of Massachusetts, 1989.

Gibson, Megan. "9 Really Strange Sports That Are No Longer in the Olympics." Time, July 6, 2012. https://olympics.time.com.

Historic New England. "African American Vacationers in New England." https://www.historicnewengland.org.

Keiper, Lauren. "'Jaws' Still Churns Waters off Martha's Vineyard." Reuters, July 7, 2010. https://www.reuters.com.

Martha's Vineyard Museum. Chris Baer. history.vineyard.net.

Massachusetts Historical Commission. "MHC Reconnaissance Survey Town Report: Oak Bluffs." 1984. https://www.sec.state.ma.us/mhc/mhcpdf/townreports/cape/oak.pdf.

Morgan, Anne. "Continuing the Tradition: African Americans on Martha's Vineyard." Huntington Theatre Company. https://www.huntingtontheatre.org/articles/Continuing-the-Tradition-African-Americans-on-Marthas-Vineyard.

MV Obsession (blog). mvobsession.com.

National Institute for Civil Discourse. University of Arizona. https://nicd.arizona.edu.

New England Historical Society. "The Green Book Guides African-Americans to Safety in New England (and Elsewhere)." newenglandhistoricalsociety.com.

Streep, Abe. "The Great White Shark Returns to Cape Cod." Outside, July 31, 2013. https://www.outsideonline.com,

Wysocki, Heather. "Oak Bluffs Reliving the Dream with Renovated Ballroom." Cape Cod Times, July 13, 2012. https://www.capecodtimes.com.

Guidebooks

Guide of Cottage City. 1879.

Illustrated New Bedford, Martha's Vineyard and Nantucket. Providence, RI: Reid Printers, 1880.

Illustrated Travel Guide. 1888.

Island Review. August 17, 1878.

Martha's Vineyard: Isle of Dreams and Health, 1932.

New York Martha's Vineyard Island Via New Haven Railroad.

Pocket Directory Guide. January 1901.

Tourist Guide of Cottage City. 1880.

Tours and Guide to Southern Massachusetts, Campground, Oak Bluffs, Vineyard Highlands and Falmouth Heights. 1868.

The Vineyard as It Was, Is, and Is to Be. 1872.

News and Periodicals

Boston Globe

Chamber of Commerce Guide

Dukes County Intelligencer/Martha's Vineyard Museum Quarterly

Ebony

Los Angeles Times

Martha's Vineyard Magazine

Martha's Vineyard Times

New York Times

Town & Country

Vineyard Gazette

About the Author

For years, Tom Dresser drove a tour bus around Martha's Vineyard. An earlier booklet, Tommy's Tour of the Vineyard (2005), followed the prescribed tourist bus route. Today, Tom offers historical walks and talks for patrons of the Pequot Hotel in Oak Bluffs. The Rise of Tourism on Martha's Vineyard is his twelfth book with The History Press.

Tom lives with his wife of twenty years, Joyce. Together they enjoy spending time with grandchildren, going for long drives, long walks and long soaks in the hot tub.

Visit thomasdresser.com or contact the author at thomasdresser@gmail.com.

Also by Thomas Dresser:
Mystery on the Vineyard
African Americans of Martha's Vineyard
The Wampanoag Tribe of Martha's Vineyard
Disaster off Martha's Vineyard
Women of Martha's Vineyard
Martha's Vineyard in World War II
Music on Martha's Vineyard
Martha's Vineyard: A History
Hidden History of Martha's Vineyard
Whaling on Martha's Vineyard
A Travel History of Martha's Vineyard

Visit us at
www.historypress.com